C0-AVX-742

THE PASTOR AT WORK IN CHRISTIAN EDUCATION

The author of this book is at present in the eleventh year of his pastorate with the Calvary Baptist Church of Norristown, Pennsylvania, a church which for many years has concerned itself with the Christian educational approach to its task. The subject-matter here may be thought of as growing directly out of his own extended practical experience. Born on the campus of a theological seminary, he is the son and grandson of a minister. His entire background is that of the parsonage. He was graduated from Bucknell University (A. B.) with the class of 1913 and from Crozer Theological Seminary (B. D.) in 1916, receiving in the same year the degree of Master of Arts from the University of Pennsylvania. Finding an increasing interest in the Christian educational task of the church, he has constantly sought to make use of the best available ideals and materials in that field. Further graduate work in Christian education at Columbia University and constant activity in almost every section of the field have served to extend his experience. Many, though not all, of the suggestions in the following chapters may be seen actually in operation in his church. A modern Christian educational building was erected there some seven years ago, housing a school of about a thousand members. The church itself has a membership of approximately twelve hundred.

THE PASTOR AT WORK IN CHRISTIAN EDUCATION

By

HENRY G. WESTON SMITH

PHILADELPHIA

THE JUDSON PRESS

CHICAGO KANSAS CITY LOS ANGELES SEATTLE

Published April, 1935
Reprinted May, 1942

Printed in U.S.A.

To

MY WIFE

WHO UNDERSTANDS
THE BACKGROUND OF IT ALL

INTRODUCTORY

In the building of modern bridges workmen are accustomed to begin simultaneously at both ends, the structure finally being joined midstream. Not so with the bridge-builders in Christian education. With them the inclination has been to put the larger force on the side of the theoretic, even though construction from the opposite shore might move slowly.

The writer of the following pages has attempted to work now at one end, now at the other. He is convinced that the force on the practical shore ought to be strengthened, that all the structure erected by the classroom is in danger of tumbling into the abyss unless builders in the local church labor bravely and soundly.

He writes, therefore, as one who believes that in the average church the strategic person in Christian education is the pastor. True, the shepherd ought not to be blamed for all the failures of the sheep, nor given credit for all their virtues; but in both directions he is far more pivotal than has yet been understood.

The ten studies here presented are therefore designed for pastors and others closely associated with them, who should further Christian education right where they are—in their own church—at once—and regardless of any obstacles they may face. An attempt has been made to approach the subject from a warmly sympathetic angle; the aim being to describe, in part, the pastor actually at work.

While a theoretic tone does not predominate, attention has been given to guarding against its violation. The desire is simply to be helpful to those who are looking for better things in the local church. It may make for greater clarity at the outset if there are listed here a few underlying assumptions.

Underlying Assumptions

1. Conditions of life have vastly changed during the past fifty—or even twenty-five—years. Since the enumeration of the items of change is a favorite first-chapter interest in many available books on Christian educational and related themes, the point is not here reargued. It seems too obvious to need arguing to people who are living in the midst of today's life.

2. The church has not wholly adapted itself to these changing conditions. Nor has any other institution. They are all "in process," and behind schedule; the church along with the rest. The author is familiar with the suggestions of certain olympians to the effect that, in Christian educational work, we should scrap "this sorry scheme of things entire," and then rebuild it "nearer to the heart's desire"; but he has not seen a rebuilt sample so convincingly constructive as to satisfy him that it was a vigorous and mature product; therefore he continues to use the existing church order. The idea is to help along the process of adaptation as rapidly and as practically as possible, beginning with an admittedly imperfect condition.

3. The church and the ministry have many points at which they can be criticized. Their present need, however, is not to be told about their failures but to be shown how they can become better. This is the need of almost every institution in society. Few have done so well as the church. Most of them are in an infinitely worse muddle. Nor is the church to be held too accountable. It is to some extent suffering from the common maladies of the society it is trying to improve. With all its limitations, it is the most hopeful factor with which to work for society's improvement.

4. With but few exceptions the pastor, who has the educational approach, has not assumed another burden additional to those which normally are his, but rather is developing a method of finally handling all the problems of his church in a more natural and easy manner than any ever yet discovered by him. Christian education is not a substitute for evangelism. It is not a substitute for anything that is good. It is a means—a method—a highway.

CONTENTS

I

THE NEW MINISTER LOOKS AT HIS TASK

1. What He Finds

No one who has not had the experience can possibly understand what emotions surge to and fro in the breast of a conscientious minister as he thinks of the church to which he is likely to go, and then at a particular moment the chairman of the pulpit committee, with a mild gesture of the left hand, says, "Well, here it is." Somehow in that phrase he seems to sense both the pride of achievement and the apology of idealism; satisfaction with the past and bewilderment regarding the future. There is an element of pathos—somewhat like that which can be detected in the voice of an unmarried uncle who, after he has held the new baby for a while, turns to the mother or the nurse and hands back the dear bundle with the feeling: "He certainly is a fine baby, but really I don't know just what to do with him."

At last, the nightmare of moving is over. The geography of the town is being learned. Names of people are unmixing themselves, and little things are happening which the pastor feels he can trust as reasonable revelations of the character of those with whom he will labor and to whom he will preach. Some who at first seemed very unpromising are proving to be of great worth; some, on the other hand, who appeared to be the very salt of the earth, are not showing themselves steady and dependable under pressure.

At the outset congregations are "good." For the present there are no serious financial problems. No one has started to criticise. Even the indigenous ill-will that exists between persons or groups in the church has taken a place of secondary importance. People are trying to make a good impression. The minister moves carefully, not taking sides in any partisan affair of traditional standing. *He would be a true minister of Jesus Christ to everyone.*

Thus gradually the qualities of the people reveal themselves. They are good; they are bad; they are weak; they are strong; wise, foolish—the same as people everywhere. They have conflicting interests among and within themselves. Basic in their lives is a great deal of perfectly natural selfishness, which frequently crops out.

Some are willing to do a high type of Christian work. Of the financially stronger people, a few are ready to be generous with their means. They love their church. In fact, a fair number of all ages, as the minister becomes acquainted with them, prove to be anxious to make their church greatly worth while to the community and the world. Some are awkward in their approach; but if they knew just how and what to do, there would be no hesitating on their part. Choice young people are ready to take responsibility, though they also are bewildered and clumsy as they consider how to go ahead.

About the time the minister is beginning to rejoice in "the hope set before him," he discovers outcroppings of personal pride, good if properly directed, but which interfere with the usefulness of those whom they color. For example, designated people have "always" held certain offices; and there is an established tradition that they must continue so to do. Certain organizations have "always" existed, and are deeply rooted in the mind and thought of those who established them —and under whose leadership in a former period they did excellent work.

When he turns to certain people with the request that they take church responsibilities involving an exact performance of duty, he discovers they are involved in social and secular pursuits which they are not willing to any great extent to surrender. Again, he finds in the church social and other groups fostered by capable and perhaps well-meaning individuals; and he can see that these very natural social groups are able to have vast influence for the right; but he becomes nervous when he realizes how at times they may fall into shortsightedness; be misguided; and, however sincere, present an administrative problem.

He finds parents who are unduly zealous for the advancement of their children in this or that phase of the work; but when he talks with them he discovers that the underlying motive is personal vanity rather than kingdom service, or even their own Christian education. Then, there are jealousies existing between persons because of events that occurred years ago. Wounds have been nursed. Hurt feelings have remained. Yet there are fine elements in the church, and he determines to do the best that can be done for everyone—good, bad, and indifferent.

He realizes that the church is a fair cross-section of the better portion of society. The very worst he does not find there, for it is not a comfortable place for them to remain. Still, he finds all kinds, or nearly all: those whose characters are excellent, those who are indifferent, the problematic. Some have brought with them into the church the base elements of the world—which supposedly they renounced when they took the covenant vow in baptism; and some are the noblest, finest, stanchest people in the world.

The minister is not deceived. He knows how great is the labor to which he has come. He feels as his Master felt when he came into the Temple, the evening of that day of Triumph, and " looked upon all things." He would enjoy withdrawing into some quiet Bethany, that the strain and stress of things might be taken from his mind, and his reordered life confess the beauty of God's peace.

2. That For Which He Longs

This young man, however, is not in the ministry for the sheer amusement he can find in it, nor for the salary. But few ministers are; with them disillusionment ultimately comes.

He longs to see progress toward the kingdom of God on earth. How difficult it is for the divine will really to be made to prevail in the hearts of men he knows full well; but he longs for the true regency of Christ, throughout industry and the economic order, throughout national life and the judiciary, throughout the whole world, that peace and fellowship may prevail. He would be a clarion voice calling for exactly the things his Saviour called for in his day, except that he would apply them to the life of the twentieth century.

Blessed are the poor in spirit . . . they that mourn . . . the meek . . . they which do hunger and thirst after righteousness . . . the merciful . . . the pure in heart . . . the peacemakers . . . they which are persecuted for righteousness sake. . .

Except your righteousness shall exceed the righteousness of the scribes and Pharisees, ye shall in no wise inherit. . .

Whosoever is angry with his brother without a cause shall be in danger of the judgment. . .

Whosoever looketh on a woman to lust after her hath already committed adultery in his heart. . .

When thou doest thine alms sound not a trumpet. . .

Lay not up for yourselves treasures upon earth. . .

First cast out the beam out of thine own eye; . .

Woe unto you . . . for ye devour widows' houses, and for a pretense make long prayers. . .

. . . Inasmuch as ye have done it unto one of the least of these my brethren ye have done it unto me. . . inasmuch as ye did it not unto one of the least of these my brethren ye did it not unto me. . .

Go ye therefore and teach all nations. . .

He sees the pulpit ministry as one means by which these things can be promoted, and is properly ambitious that he may never disappoint hungering souls who come to the sanctuary with hope that they may learn of Christ. He desires to be known as a preacher whose sermons instruct, inspire, convert and thrill darkened and discouraged lives. He feels that, after all, the pulpit is still at the center of the work of the Christian ministry; he knows that the man who consistently preaches great sermons must consistently live a great life. Sermons do not just happen. They are the product of Gethsemanes, Galilees, temple courts, but also of scores upon scores of hidden hours about which the world can never know. He understands what sweating of blood it will cost to make his pulpit a center of power; but he believes the ambition a worthy one, and holds to it. Can he measure up? He wonders. Yet he is resolute.

Being a child of the present world he knows how complex are the influences around each of his hearers—and how subtle. He knows that, though a person does learn by hearing the word of truth, the more emphatic influences come from seeing and doing. *Only when thought is put into action is it most powerful.* He therefore builds in his mind a picture of his church organized for action. He himself wants to be a soul-winner, a teacher, a worker; but just as earnestly he wants the entire church organized, trained and inspired for these ends.

How can so many people be organized and trained, even granted they are vaguely willing? Has anyone in the church sufficient vision, purpose, and time to take the task off his hands? He hopes; but finally is convinced that through friendly conference, diplomacy, and sheer executive ability, he must be the leader of the entire organized life of the church. To such an end he must set aside large blocks of time. He sees he must develop his powers as a presiding officer, as a writer of countless letters, and as a propagandist of the gospel through local church printed matter and local papers.

He has perceived the modern scientific trend in all cultural things, including Christian education. Being a child of the present schools he has no desire to abandon scientific attitudes and methods, *if they are in thorough good faith.* But he is no longer jumping at conclusions. He has observed in his own heart and in the lives of people everywhere the utter sterility —the pathetic deadness—of a life that does not know the meaning of personal Christian experience. Therefore, while he is enthusiastic in his desire to be a good teacher of religion, he is just as determined to be a real personal-evangelist, quickening individuals of all ages to Christian decision. He wants to become, in the original New Testament sense, a " fisher of men."

And then, as he visualizes the people of his parish, varying, as they do, in age, social status, mentality and physique, he enters again into the feelings of his Lord who, in that other time looked upon other multitudes of people. He sees them as " sheep without a shepherd." He longs to be with them in their homes; to share their burdens and joys; to accompany them through life's terrific experiences; to minister unto them when they are sick or in trouble; to bring them back when they have wandered astray; to be, in short, all that a good shepherd should be to his flock.

If the church is of any considerable size (above 600 members, for example), he has to face the fact that unless he can delegate much desk and administrative detail to a secretary, or director of Christian education, or both, the time element will severely limit his parish visitation. Constant calling in the average local field must and can be done. It is needful to the people, and to the minister as well. Under no circumstances will a sensible minister turn it off with a disdainful and superior shrug of the shoulders, as much as to say: " I can't bother with that sort of silly thing." It is not silly; it is vital; and he knows it.

But he surely does have to realize that with administrative, supervisory, and desk details multiplying as they do in the larger church, he will be bound to perform less than the whole task in the pulpit, supervisory and administrative sections of his vocation; or else in the matter of urgent and special calling; or else in regular house-to-house visitation. The task must be divided, shifted, shared by others. He must have substantial help.

On his desk is the little book, *The Minister and His Opportunity,* by Frederick A. Agar. This careful student of the pastoral task has some rather important convictions about pastoral calling:

> Next . . . comes the minister's care of the sick, the afflicted, and the unsaved. The minister is a specialist in spiritual realms. The sick, the afflicted, and the unsaved need the help of such a specialist. Such work is trying to the minister's soul and wearying to his body, but out of it come experiences that give point to his preaching and illustrations for the teaching of God's Word and ways. There is so much of this kind of work that the average pastor is always confronted with a demand that he is unable to satisfy, with the time and strength at his command.
>
> The average minister spends from fourteen to sixteen hours each day at work, yet the work is never completed, as many of his tasks require constant repetition. It will doubtless be noticed that no mention of house-to-house calling upon church-members has been made in this study of a minister's primary tasks. Church-members, as a rule, expect a minister to call upon them, and absent themselves from church or cancel their subscriptions when he fails to do so. Even in a small church, if the minister spends his time in attendance upon the well members of his church it is certain he is neglecting some more important phases of work. The membership of the church should regularly participate in the ministries of their house of worship and thus keep in contact with their pastor. They should set him free from calling upon them because others, inside and outside the church, who are sick and afflicted, really need him. The selfish demand for personal attention from the

minister often results in depriving someone in the hospital, or kept at home by trouble, from his ministry. He has not time to see everybody. Many an unsaved person stays out of the Kingdom and the church because the pastor is so rushed with secondary tasks that he cannot take advantage of such primary opportunities as dealing with unsaved people. What does the average pastoral call accomplish, after all, unless there is sickness or affliction with which to deal? It doubtless pleases the pride of some selfish church-member, but it wastes some valuable time of the pastor and, therefore, should not be continued. *If continuous pastoral calling is to cease, the pastor must not be expected to take the initiative in the matter. The resulting criticism will be too great for him to face alone. The lay church leaders should take the responsibility and change the situation in behalf of their minister.*

The minister, whatever may be his present point of view with regard to the problem here discussed, may as well face the fact that he must take some position in his own mind and work toward the final realization of it; for what he is able to do with pastoral calling, and the manner in which he handles it, will have a strong influence in either aiding his whole ministry from every angle or constantly "throwing dust in his eyes."

It is the present writer's personal conviction, after painstaking and long-continued study of the problem, that in the larger church the ideal situation is one in which the pastor is furnished with a staff of from one to three or more half-time or full-time paid assistants who can constantly relieve him of all secretarial and much administrative and detail work, so that he can do somewhat more calling than seems to be implied in the above quotation. While the needs of various parishes differ, the usual situation could be helped by a more generous (if wisely conducted) calling plan. It will be noted that the special calls of which Doctor Agar speaks, in the average church of more than 600 members, will never be less than fifteen or twenty a week, and will usually average between thirty and fifty a week, or even more than that. This being the case, it seems to be the minister's place to have been in each home at least one or more times so that he can carry in his mind the spiritual picture of each family. Beyond that it is his duty and privilege to go as far as he can without impoverishing his study life and ministry of preaching, or sacrificing the thoroughness of his leadership as an administrator, supervisor and inspiring spirit of the church program of Christian education. If he does not have the assistants needful at his beck and call, the analysis given by Doctor Agar is unquestionably correct. That is, he should not be permitted to attempt a regular round of house-to-house calling. He may be able to do it, but it will certainly be at the expense of other things. We say, "should not be permitted," by which we mean that his official boards should protect him by a systematic plan of educating the people against "running him to death." The reader, however, should be fully informed of Doctor Agar's proposed solution of the problem presented by the need of constant house-to-house calling. He suggests an official board large enough and faithful enough to constantly cover the whole constituency and thus keep reporting to the pastor the cases needing special pastoral attention. He would not have less calling done. He would have much more done. This is the old principle of the Wesleyan "Class Leader," in which, each week or each month, the leader reports with regard to the spiritual condition of all in his class. Doctor Agar's analysis is a thoroughly sound one. Let the pastor, however, be very wise in his method of presenting it to his official board. They must accept and lead the way or he will have hard going.

In the apportioning of his administrative calling time the minister soon realizes there are some people to whom special attention may well be given because of their value to the work. They are his inner circle of leaders; like the Twelve.

But if this inner circle is not his official group in church and school, then he knows he will do well either to bring them gradually into his official group, or rebuild his "inner circle." Normally he will not expect to prosper in the work indefinitely unless there is a special friendliness between himself and his official family. It just will not work out unless he can have the honest, friendly confidence of the majority of those who are the elected representatives of the church. It is not that he is making favorites of them; he is simply cultivating those whom the church has by regular vote designated as "favorites."

Closely related to the important but endless task of pastoral calling is the very heavy duty of attendance upon the many meetings in connection with the life of the church, the life of the community and the life of the related organizations in the church, such as organized classes, guilds, brotherhoods, and women's societies. These meetings are of varying importance so far as their rightful demand upon his time is concerned. Certain central board meetings, really strategic in planning and directing the work of the church, should find him always present unless there is an unusually important hindrance. The major services of the church and school he will of course attend. That is understood. But when it comes to the many smaller meetings of an every-month or every-week character his schedule should be drawn very carefully. Once or twice each year he should, if possible, visit these smaller groups. It should not be expected of him that he will be able to do more than this. He can not be in everything. Let the work be departmentalized and go on under its own leaders. That is what they are for. The pastor comes in only "on occasion." More than this should not be expected, except as the pastor of his own free choice increases the visits.

Again, the minister has entered upon this work with a resolute determination to bridge the gap between the ideals and theories of Christian education on the one hand and the conditions in the local church on the other. He believes in "The Seven Objectives" [1] *and will constantly test his work by them:*

I. God

Religious education seeks to foster in growing persons a consciousness of God as a reality in human experience, and a sense of personal relationship to him.

II. The Saviour

Religious education seeks to develop in growing persons such an understanding and appreciation of the personality, life, and teachings of Jesus as will lead to discovery of him as Saviour and Lord, loyalty to him and his cause, and manifest itself in daily life and conduct.

III. Christlike Character

Religious education seeks to foster in growing persons a progressive and continuous development of Christlike character.

IV. Christian Social Order

Religious education seeks to develop in growing persons the ability and disposition to participate in and contribute constructively to the building of a social order embodying the ideal of the fatherhood of God and the brotherhood of man.

V. The Church

Religious education seeks to develop in growing persons the ability and disposition to participate in the organized society of Christians—the church.

VI. A Christian Philosophy of Life

Religious education seeks to lead growing persons into: A Christian interpretation of life and the universe; the ability to see in it God's purpose and plan; a life philosophy built on this interpretation.

[1] Adopted by the International Council of Religious Education, and printed in a bulletin entitled *The Development of a Curriculum of Religious Education.*

VII. Christian History

Religious education seeks to effect in growing persons the assimilation of the best religious experience of the race, as effective guidance to present experience.

Perhaps it will be best not to put these rather high-sounding statements before the people in just these words; but the pastor does hope to realize the objectives, in concrete form.

He is anxious, moreover, to be a good example to everyone; as father, husband, leader, friend; exhibiting in what he does and is the qualities he wishes to teach. It has disturbed him that not all ministers are thus distinguished. He wants to know and love everyone, showing favor to none and fear of none. He wants to be a counselor to everyone. He wants so to arrange his habits of life as to conserve his strength and health. This will make him useful through many years. He exercises the very natural and reasonable hope that he may properly educate his children, and at least in some measure protect his family from the bugbear of utter financial dependence in old age—if old age should be reached.

He desires, in short, to be every inch a Christian minister; all aspects of his work being thoroughly real. He does not see his gospel as a thing unrelated to the problems of today. Quite otherwise. He is determined to remain a prophet of righteousness, in the true Old Testament sense, making permanent his nation's life by making practical his nation's religion.

3. That Which He May Fairly Expect

But how can he reasonably expect to do all these things? Any one of them is a task so great as to absorb his full time and strength. He is only one man. By forcing his heart, nerve and sinew beyond moderation he may be able to do twice as much as seems humanly possible; but in more than that it is unlikely he will long hold out. Some thing—perhaps many things—will be poorly done.

Our minister knows he is facing an utterly superhuman task. For perfection he can not reasonably hope, and the sooner he understands this the better it will be for his work. To look for perfection and then to experience such limitations as are inevitable, may break his spirit. He must therefore know that it is for him to strive for a reasonable progress toward the ideal.

No phase of all this work is without its religious educational effect. For that reason one finds it necessary to survey the whole task of the pastor—in the matter of Christian education. Some things, to be sure, are more important than others. He must constantly decide in what ratio he will devote himself to each phase of his task; and even then he must know that he will not see his full dream come into actuality.

His is, indeed, a big task—so very big it needs make him most humble and courageous. He must never surrender his idealism nor abandon hope. He must go toward his ideal of accomplishment as far as possible, ever trying to lift his people to the high levels of "ought," "should" and "will." And in everything he must maintain the "Castle of his Soul," whither he can frequently retreat and having shut fast the door commune with the great and good and wise of all ages. Here is certainly to be found his *sine qua non,* "without-which-never!"

And now that we have looked at the new minister and watched him survey his task, a multitude of voices in chorus will cry: "But we are not new ministers. We only wish we were. We want to move but can not. Economic stress has made it seem well for us to go; but just as certainly it has made it impossible for us to find new places into which we could fit. What are we to do?"

Bless our hearts! It is essentially the same thing. Each year requires that we shall look over our work again, as if it were a brand new task, and then go forward with the zest of one who is beginning a pastorate instead of a day. Nothing is so powerful as this in the direction of removing pressure.

The angel is there in the marble. Snatch up the stone. Release the smiling face!

For years it had been trampled in the street
Of Florence by the drift of heedless feet—
The stone that star-touched Michael Angelo
Turned to that marble loveliness we know.

You mind the tale—how he was passing by
When the rude marble caught his Jovian eye,
That stone men had dishonored and had thrust
Out to the insult of the wayside dust.
He stooped to lift it from its mean estate,
And bore it on his shoulder to the gate,
Where all day long a hundred hammers rang.
And soon his chisel round the marble sang,
And suddenly the hidden angel shone:
It had been *waiting* prisoned in the stone.

Thus came the cherub with the laughing face
That long has lighted up an altar-place.[2]

—*Edwin Markham.*

A few months before this material was to go to press, the author heard a rather unique message given by the general superintendent of a Sunday church school, as he addressed his executive committee, composed of administrative officers and departmental superintendents, meeting for the first time after vacation and at the beginning of the new school year. It was the seventeenth year of his active service as their superinten-

[2] From *The Gates of Paradise and Other Poems.* Copyrighted by Edwin Markham and used with his permission.

dent, and he was searching for a means of truthfully envisioning for them and with them the great and incomplete task. A portion of his statement follows:

As we enter upon the work of the School in its *Golden Anniversary* year, I would like you to think of me tonight as a *new* general superintendent, inexperienced and unfamiliar with the requirements of office, but having an open mind and being anxious to raise the standard of accomplishments of the school. I hope you will assume the attitude of helpfulness toward me as you would toward anyone else entering for the first time upon these important duties; that you will be willing to share with me the benefits of your knowledge, thought and experience; and that you will contribute to the work the full measure of your capacities, in order to overcome my deficiencies due to lack of training and experience.

As your "new" general superintendent I should like to add that I am well acquainted with my predecessor, having closely observed his work during the past few years. I feel there is opportunity for marked improvement in the achievements of the office as he has held it. I appeal to you to assist me, by suggestion and by the sharing of responsibilities, to lead the school to achieve greater results than have been possible heretofore.

I think I should also tell you of an important decision I made during the past week, as an evidence of my purpose to devote to the school a major portion of my time, not required in the discharge of my duties to the corporation with which I am employed in an executive capacity; and to use my abilities to the best advantage possible in the general administration of the school.

During the past year I took over the farm which for more than 125 years has been in the possession of my family. On account of sentiment, and the opportunity for the development of a profitable side-enterprise, I have been debating for months the necessity of making an adjustment in my interests, which include: my position with the corporation; my supervision of farm operations; and my leadership of the Bible school. I am not in position to sacrifice the income from my corporate employment, and am not in possession of the wealth necessary to carry the obligation of the luxury of "a gentleman's farm." After due consideration I decided, during the last few days, to accept an offer of sale which will eliminate the responsibility for the farm and enable me to devote my time to earning an income and assuming active leadership in Christian education.

As a result of special attention to my physical condition in recent years I am ready to enter upon the new duties in full vigor of health and with keen enthusiasm for the work to which I am called, realizing the great need for Christian education and recognizing the opportunity this position offers for a worth-while Christian service.

Certainly, such a statement as this is—in the best sense of the term *challenging*—not only to volunteer workers who have long been active, but also to pastors who in their local tasks have felt "the burden and heat of the day."

II

ORGANIZATIONS AND TRADITIONS

"Like unto a man that is a householder, who bringeth forth out of his treasure things new and old" (Matthew 13: 52).

The typical church program is not perfect. A pastor discovers this before he has been on his field three weeks—or even three hours. In print the description of what is sometimes regarded as an *ideal field* reads as though here were the very anteroom to heaven; but in actuality it is only a tolerably good church with certain excellent points. Together with these are customs and methods as old and outworn as an ancient beaver hat. Educational method at its best is imperfect. The writer has become fairly conversant with a number of the most notable churches in the country. He has been careful to recognize their excellencies; but has always turned away to confess to himself that, if he were to list these places by name, cataloging under each its specific imperfections and needs, he would certainly at once be written down as the most heartless iconoclast—the most brutal critic.

To admit this, however, one does not have to be ungracious. Indeed there is no way to avoid the admission, if progress is to be more than a phantom of which one expects now and then to have an evanescent glimpse. Where there is no humble sense of need there is likely to be no advance. Self-satisfaction never brought in the Kingdom.

1. Tradition as Education

But with this conviction of need there must always go an appreciation of what is already there. Rarely is it possible for a person to be effective as a leader of those whom he holds in contempt. Nor has the ministry always been free from such an attitude.

The traditions one encounters in the local parish have consumed a long time in their growth. Once developed they give a kind of character to the church. Each oncoming generation is schooled in them, and the message of any specific church comes in good measure by means of these traditions. As a matter of fact, it is ultimately discovered by every discerning leader that tradition is a very powerful, and all in all, wholesome means of educating the oncoming church. If the body of traditions, therefore, is good, the church at the very outset has an invaluable educational asset. If it is bad, obviously the institution is under a serious initial handicap.

To improve the traditions of a church, therefore, is highly important. Here is a little society, a little world in itself. It has a history, a spirit, a body of attitudes, a reputation, an atmosphere, which it tends constantly to stamp upon all who come under its influence. Why? Simply because each one of these traditions serves as a sort of whip, keeping leaders in line and determining what they shall tell the remainder of the people. No matter what some may say about their "independence from tradition," by it they are always both helped and hindered—and that very powerfully. It restrains. It drives on. It eddies, swirls and sweeps like a mighty stream whose course cannot easily be changed, but whose forces, if skilful hands start them in a different direction, cut a new channel as deep as the old. The question always is, When should the current be turned into new channels, and when should it keep to the old?

Here, for example, is the public worship of the church. In one place there will be a strong Sunday morning service, but a rather weak Sunday night service; and yet a few blocks away will be found another church in which, for some reason, the exact reverse is true. People have come to *expect* things to be that way in these two churches. Those planning and those supporting are by tradition strongly stimulated to a maintenance of practically the status quo. Either condition can be utterly reversed; but it will take an extended time to break down the expectation of the people that things will continue to be as they are, and to set up the expectation that they will be different. The entire congregation is unconsciously working for that which they have come to know as "the way we do in this church."

Or here are the various missionary organizations. The women's society has perhaps been a constant factor. Even it, however, is subject to the good and bad influences of tradition. Once let the people of the church acquire the impression that the society is an unimportant factor, and an unimportant factor it is likely to be. It seems that all join together in carrying out the reputation it has. On the other hand, let it but get the name for worth and good sense—it is just as sure to continue to be characterized by these things. All join in that process.

Similarly with young people's, or children's, missionary groupings. Each has its history, its personnel, its entrenched program—the reputation that it "has always been this way."

Let no pastor think the traditions having to do with one age-group in a given church have nothing to do with the church as a whole. A wise or foolish move with regard to a children's organization may reverberate with a voice of thunder (and the effect of lightning!) in the women's society, the Sunday school, the young people's society, or even in one or both of the official boards of the church. Wherever else the influence extends, it is almost certain to be noted in the general public worship. Here *everything* registers, whether by increasing or decreasing attendance, or by conditioning the "atmosphere." The position in which the pastor finds himself, then, is difficult. He is like a physician whose business it is not only to find the cure for some trifling cold or mild germ infection, but also to prescribe diet, tonic and exercise calculated to keep the patient fit; and in some instances there will be found organic difficulties that require the skilful hand of a surgeon. When this is the case in the church it may be well for the pastor to refresh his memory with the knowledge that the best surgeons are careful to get the patient's confidence and good-will; that they are very particular about the treatment of the wound, before and after, so that no infection with damaging results may follow; and that the giving of the anesthetic is now known to be a special skill of the utmost importance. Perhaps his is not the hand to wield the knife. Perhaps it is. More often he will be the attending physician.

There are, then, in this entire connection at least two propositions worthy of careful consideration:

2. Two Propositions

(1) *In building a better organization for Christian educational purposes in the local church a gradual modification of existing plans and methods often moves more rapidly toward the goal than a violent revolution.*

There will be those who differ with this proposition. Some who have had much experience may be convinced that the slow method is too slow. As a rule, however, an experienced and observant person will be inclined to feel that, with comparatively few exceptions, the less fuss and noise made about reforms, the better. Revolution, take it all in all, is a dirty, dusty, crude sort of thing. Whether in national, in family, or in church life, it leaves much to be cleaned up, brushed down and rearranged; and even then there remain stains and scars that are beyond repair.

The point is that no matter how imperfect the organized Christian educational factors in a church, they are with few exceptions the result of good will. Each of these societies, guilds, boards or classes, each of the customs and methods, at one time grew out of a sincere sense of need. The desire was to set up a plan of work that would function helpfully toward a definite and worthy end. At the time it was very likely the best plan, in view of the knowledge in hand and the leadership available. It served a noble purpose. For that it is to be honored. Anything to displace it must give clear evidence it will actually work better. It is not entirely a question of how it sounds, or who has recommended it, or whether it is "the latest thing in the educational world." You see this improvement that is being attempted must not only be good. It must commend itself to others as being good. It must win their loyalty and enthusiasm. A poor plan with a person enthusiastic about it may achieve more real Christian education than a better plan with a person who is half-hearted, and wounded about it.

No pastor ever lost time, then, by being sympathetic with and appreciative of those who had gone before him. The organizations which he found on his arrival cannot with impunity be frowned upon as though they were absurd and fantastic relics of a day when people were well-meaning but benighted. Their best spirit must be caught and marked. What are the functions, the purposes, the aims which they now have, in view of their earlier spirit and purpose? How can one more forward step be added to many that already have been taken? Those people were pioneers. Lucky for us! We would not today have what we have if they had not been face-forward.

> Was the Mayflower launched by cowards,
> Steered by men behind their time?
> Turn those tracks toward Past or Future,
> That make Plymouth Rock sublime?

And today we are simply trying to be true to the noble traditions which we have found written into the best of our history.

Such an attitude is in no sense for mere effect. It is reasonable and honest appreciation. The former generation elementally was just as pioneering as the present; and the present elementally is just as noble as the past. It is only a matter of each appreciating the other and realizing that each is the complement of the other.

Patience, then! Not too many steps at once! An occasional restudy, or "survey" (though that formidable word "survey" has strangled many an infant reform), if conducted in a thoroughly sympathetic spirit by well selected people, may decidedly hasten improvement. The work, the "functioning," however, can often be improved more readily than the constitutions. Very well. So let it be. Improve the working and then bring the constitutions up to the level of the work.

If constitutions prove to be a menace because they are in print—and there are sticklers for "the printed law"—though patience is necessary, it is important to remember that it is really not the constitution that impedes; it is the spirit of the sticklers. If somehow they can be led to see the deeper purposes of the constitution, they themselves may become liberals in constitutional law, or even aspire to a recodification of the whole thing. The more one sees of people, the more one is inclined to believe that human stumbling-blocks within the church are that way not because of deliberate malice, or intentional reaction, but because they have not seen a better way. They are honestly not convinced. Jealousy and personal antagonism dating back to some former conflict are of course often a factor, and may blind the eyes and stop the ears of people who otherwise would be very discerning. But with these factors eliminated the real problem is to enlighten the people through a guileless process of study concerning the deeper spirit and purpose of the existent organizations.

The proposition that organizations are always ready to adapt themselves to changing conditions will usually be accepted. This is all that is needful. The automobile is an adaptation of the ox-cart. A skyscraper is an adaptation of a cave, or the limb of a tree; perhaps a combination of the two. He who in boasting of present mechanical achievements denies that they are the outgrowth of a long struggle upward and claims that the present generation can take all the credit—well, "the truth is not in him." So too, he who fails to see that the best plans for the church of tomorrow are to be found in seed form in the church of yesterday and the day before, is not only unrealistic, but also a poor student of human nature.

Modification and adaptation, and not revolution, are the best high-speed methods of building a better organization in the Christian church.

Our second proposition is:

(2) *The pastor must not be reconciled to conditions as they are. He must lead the people forward. He must see defects when defects are present and gently but persistently strive for their correction.*

The Sunday church school was organized when community life was utterly different from what it is today. The missionary organizations may have come into being before the time of hectic week-day programs, "engagements," now so familiar to parents of boys and girls of school age. The automobile, the motion-picture, the radio, commuting parents, bridge clubs, high-speed business life . . . all of these things, as suggested in our preliminary assumptions, were not in the picture so short a time ago as twenty or twenty-five years, or were not so insistent and demanding.

There are usually supposed to be only two things that can

be done. One is to "hold the fort" on the present plan without changing the policy; close one's eyes to the facts, and refuse to adapt to the extent of a single inch. Often this course is followed, heroically, under great discouragement, with partially satisfactory results. Sometimes the results are depressing in the extreme. The other course is to surrender to conditions and have a popular and successful organization, largely "sold out" to the world in which it finds itself, and buying its success at the price of character. "We have to do the thing that will draw the people." But there is a third course, better than either of these. It is to analyze the new conditions that have to be met in view of the highest and finest purposes which the organization has had; and then strive to adapt those purposes to existing needs. It will not be easy. Anyone who faces forward, and tries persistently to lead people forward, will find that he is subject to criticism and misunderstanding. While this should make a leader gentle it must not "scare him out." When the pastor is sure he knows exactly where he is going in leading the people forward, it is his supreme call from God to "speak to the children of Israel that they go forward." The Red Sea and some wanderings may be ahead; but he is the leader, and a leader must lead. Changes have to be made constantly. None must be made unnecessarily or without purpose. It seems only human, and certainly it is a fact, that a church will be slow to forgive its pastor if he is unwise in too many of his decisions. Where personnel or organization plans are involved, his score for correct decisions must be especially good.

But the pastor must somehow go ahead. If he is likely to incur criticism for aggressiveness, he must also face the fact that he will be criticized for allowing things to drift along a path of inaction. He is the prophet. He is the shepherd. He should see, as no one else, how the program of the church in its Christian educational aspects is influenced by the habits and conditions of life which are *right now* deeply entrenched

Inherite
Year ahead

; Time makes ancient good uncouth;
nward, who would keep abreast of

ires! we ourselves must Pilgrims be,
er boldly through the desperate win-

l with the Past's blood-rusted key."

III

ENGENDERING THE SPIRIT OF CHRISTIAN EDUCATION

Every minister has his own way of working, and "by and large" should work only in that way. One will establish a stronghold in preaching; another, in faithful parish visitation; another, in the development and management of a proper organization; another, as a worker with children. But if a man is convinced that he should give himself to an extended pastorate which takes for its dominant motive the fostering of Christian education among all his people, he will soon discover that he has to do reasonably well in many other capacities. While he may do wisely to build his leadership around some distinguishing gift by means of which he can gain prestige, he dare not count upon this alone. He is seeking a sustained and even leadership. This requires the good-faith meeting of needs as they are discovered among people whose lives are infinitely various. If a minister is asked what is the best center around which to build, he is likely to reply at once, "The pulpit." But he will pause to hope he has not been misunderstood.

1. The Pulpit

Whether the pastor has before him a throng or only "the faithful few," they are the bone and muscle of his church. So much is happening every week in his life and theirs—and so much has to happen—that he must find at least this every-week opportunity to pour out to them his soul's longings. Otherwise he and they will so widely diverge in thought that unity of purpose will be beyond the bounds of reasonable hope.

By "the pulpit" one of course means to include the mid-week service. These occasions are his supreme opportunity, when the responsive ones in the church expose themselves to such contagion as he is ready to communicate.

But he cannot infect them with that which he himself does not possess. As we come in contact with pastors from a rather wide variety of churches, meeting them in conventions, conferences and clubs, we are not likely to be overwhelmingly impressed with their clear comprehension of the theory and practice of Christian education in the local church. The competent among them in this respect seem to be quite in the minority. If this impression be correct, it is a serious matter, for the pastor who does not know his field from the angle of Christian education must face the fact that he does not know his field as he should. To speak plainly, the range of his special study for the next year or two is clearly marked out. He should lose no time in selecting materials and going at it.

He will have a delightful time as he engages in this task. He may turn his attention thither with the thought that he is leaving some more enjoyable field—doctrinal, philosophical, psychological, sociological, historical, literary. Quite the opposite. Preaching should begin with the needs of people rather than with paragraphs of books. Theology, philosophy, history, literature, can never be worthy of the minister's attention if their study does not spring from and illuminate the experiences and lives that make up his church's constituency. Some of the best teachers of homiletics are today using the term, "project preaching," to describe a type of pulpit method that begins with felt needs in the lives of the people and moves from this point in the direction of such illustrative matter, Scripture and doctrines as prove their truth by their pragmatic usefulness.

With such an approach it is quite amazing how the conventional reading diet of the minister will suddenly gain a new flavor. All that is worth while in that which he has formerly read now appears in a new order and new connection, and perhaps even under a slightly different name. It is now something that grows out of developing human souls. He centers his attention, for example, upon the few basic ideas that appeal to and help the growing Christian experience of four- and five-year-old children. Suddenly he discovers he has a course of interesting and helpful sermons for any age. He turns to graded materials prepared to meet the needs of junior-age boys and girls; and behold he is suddenly saying to himself that here are more important doctrines, more interestingly presented, than he has come upon in many a month of head-breaking reading of a technical adult character. Or again, he turns to the lesson materials prepared for intermediate, or senior and young people's groups, and finds himself saying: "Why, this is the best and most orderly presentation of the essentials of Christian doctrine that I have discovered in a long time. Here is material for a full year of extremely helpful study and preaching. The great truths are now presented to me in terms of actual life!"

And he is right. The zest of true Christian education is coming upon him. Henceforth his preaching will be enlivened by the vivid stories and experiences he has found in the plain Sunday church school lessons as prepared for the various ages. Furthermore, he will turn from these to the journals, "leaders," and numerous books, all of which touch his task from interpretative or informative angles. Here again, without going outside the one distinctive field, he will find it has covered or touched all the varied aspects of his ministry.

He will be so absorbed with the urgent matters of growing Christian lives under his care that he will simply *have* to keep away from controversial and divisive matters that "eat as doth a gangrene"—and cannot possibly come to any great good. He will devote himself to the rich but simple truths of Christian ways of living and believing; and his ministry will lengthen because each year there will still remain so much that he would like to help the people do and be.

2. Pastoral

While the pulpit is the point of beginning, it is of course only that. The assignment and description of tasks nearly always becomes in large measure a person to person matter. It seems that a minister must look directly into the eyes of another, picture the same need which he may have pictured many times before in his preaching or worship program, describe the kind of a worker needed, and then quietly and persuasively say, "You are the one for this task." This will be done through pastoral calls, by or without special appointment, and through scheduled conferences at the parsonage or church office. If the service in question is one of permanent responsibility, the interview regarding it should be appropriately dignified by the arrangement of a special conference. If it is a departmental superintendency, for example, neither the pastor nor the general superintendent[1] will feel like making the approach alone. They will do it together, and may even have called in a third person to act as an interested partner. The occasion will have as its objective the recruiting of a leader. An important by-product, however, will be an engendering of the spirit of Christian education in the three persons present. We say "three," because the pastor will find his own understanding of the work growing with every such conference. As he and the general superintendent try to teach others they will themselves be learning.

[1] Throughout these studies the term "general superintendent" designates the general superintendent of the Sunday church school. "Departmental superintendent" designates a superintendent of one of the departments of the Sunday church school; as primary, intermediate, adult.

In Chapter I we recognized the difficulty, especially in larger churches, of doing all the house-to-house visitation a pastor wishes to do. By house-to-house visitation, however, we meant to indicate the indiscriminate calling that is arranged to "cover the parish twice a year." Most of one's afternoons, however, ought to be spent out in the parish with a fair proportion of the time devoted to calls that aim to teach the people how to improve upon the work they are doing; or that aim to discover how the minister himself can improve upon the work *he* is doing. If these personal contacts in the homes of the people are not constantly made, problems—misunderstandings—are bound to arise. Once they have arisen the visitation becomes imperative and of immediate importance. It is the quickest avenue of progress, and though it requires effort, grace and tact, it is the "least expensive" course to follow. Except in unusual cases, people still respond to frank kindliness.

The pastor must know exactly what he wishes the prospective worker to do; or how he wishes the present worker to improve. They will ask him regarding details. He must not hesitate or evade. They expect him to know, if not details of program material, at least where these may be secured. If he is wise he will have secured the materials in advance, and have them ready at the strategic moment to place in the hands of the worker. He will use no deception or trickery in order to "put something over" on the person with whom he is speaking; but he will understand that there is a good and a poor way to persuade people; and he will try to use at least as good skill in recruiting Christian workers as he would use if he were selling radiator brushes. In his work for the Master, in other words, he should use a first-class technique. With such an approach, whether he wins his leader or not, at this particular time, he will have engendered the spirit of true Christian service.

At conventions, conferences and institutes, he will be with his group, sharing in these affairs and conveying to those whom he has arranged to have present the feeling of deep respect he has for any honest effort to learn how to become more proficient in teaching the way to Christ. He will have counseled with them, before going or en route, as to what subjects are most important for each, and how the group can best divide its attentions, and why. He may take these occasions to call attention to specific hopes and ambitions he has concerning the work in their church, and how this particular conference or convention can serve to prepare for a special part or special parts of their program for the coming year or years.

A discreet use of books or magazine articles among selected people can also prove very effective in building the educational atmosphere. One finds that if he hands a particular book to a definite person, asking him if *he* would not like to read it sometime within the next two weeks—" after which I should like to have Mrs. Blank read it "—there will usually be an immediate response. A note in the front of the book with blank spaces for the names of those who have read it might help.

Clippings from the Christian educational journals, mailed to key-persons with a brief personal note attached, will create an occasion for discussion of a principle when reception of the note and clipping is acknowledged orally, as it very likely will be.

All these pastoral means of engendering the spirit of Christian education seem slow. There apparently is no method of growing oaks over night. The growth of the Kingdom is even so; it is slow. " Precept upon precept, precept upon precept; line upon line, line upon line; here a little, there a little." Jesus never said that the Kingdom of God would be like a whirlwind, or a sky-rocket, or a balloon-ascension. He said it would be like seed planted in the earth, like leaven in a lump of dough.

3. An Inner Circle

Eventually there will have to be an inner circle of congenial spirits upon whom the pastor can reckon as real coworkers in the strategy of a perennial evangelism, educationally viewed. Normally the details of his work will be so endlessly multiplied that he will simply be overwhelmed by them. In sheer exhaustion or confusion he will begin to "let things slip." Associates will help him to guard against this. He can not be everywhere at one time. He can not indoctrinate everyone at once. He will therefore early set himself to the special teaching of a group of leaders who will as nearly as possible duplicate his efforts. At certain points they should even greatly surpass his efforts.

He will frankly tell them how difficult and how endless he finds the task of Christian education in the local church; that he is turning to them under the stress of necessity, because he knows full well that he himself can do only a fragment of it. Together they will outline some reading—not too much at a time—and come to a few clear tentative conclusions as to what is the special field of Christian education, and what are the feasible steps now to be taken.

In setting his mind upon an inner circle upon whom to concentrate his hope he will be both practical and Scriptural; practical, because it is the admittedly efficient method of working in all organizations; Scriptural, because it was the method of Isaiah, of John the Baptist, of Jesus and of Paul.

It may be well to have several such inner circles. For example, there will be his Sunday church school staff, including just the official leaders. They are most actively and intimately tied up with the educational work and furnish an immediate opportunity. They have wrestled with their tasks and, if they are made of the right character-stuff, will be ready for help from any source. He will naturally begin here, for if he cannot lead these, who are actively in the work, he will surely have difficulty in leading any others. Yet exactly that may be the case—a problem which will be taken up in Chapter IV.

Normally, then, the staff meeting of the Sunday church school will be regarded as an opportunity to reach an inner circle. Except in unusual cases the head of this staff will not be the pastor but the general superintendent. Yet the pastor, if he knows his field and his people, without saying too much can say just the right thing at the right time to guide the entire group in its deliberations. His preliminary conferences with the general superintendent will have made it unnecessary to say too much, for the superintendent and he will be in perfect agreement before the meeting begins. Furthermore, the discussion and reports that he hears at these meetings will reveal to him many things yet undone, or at best only poorly done. He will have his note-book and pencil at hand to take down memoranda of matters to be attended to "tomorrow afternoon" in the course of the calling period; other matters for private, personal conference with the general superintendent, or this or that departmental superintendent; and so on. If there is not such a thing as a staff meeting in addition to the general workers' conference, the pastor will of course make it his first work to teach the general superintendent the value and need of such a thing. He may even temporarily conduct it; but will probably feel this is not so wise as helping the superintendent plan the program for it, so that he (the pastor) can be a sort of general adviser of them all. *But, mark you! he must know his field.* He must always be the star student of his whole inner circle. The work in which these people are engaged is far too great and difficult to be fully mastered by anyone, once for all. It is a matter of constant study for him as well as for them.

In addition to the staff of the school, however, it is likely he will feel the need of something in the nature of a board of Christian education, authorized by the church, with the function of guiding all the educational plans of the church and school. It need not be a large group numerically; but it should have the authority of the entire church back of it. There is only one thing to be guarded against with this board, it must not be a hindrance. Better not have any such board and "muddle along" as well as possible with the problems of coordination, than to have a board which does not know and have the spirit of its task. We have seen Christian education committees and boards of Christian education appointed because that was the popularly recommended thing to have; but they really did not know the first thing about the work over which they had authority. Such situations are tragic. Far better none at all. Such a committee or board is created and maintained for two distinct reasons: (1) To coordinate the various Christian educational agencies in the church; to suggest wise adjustments that will overcome duplications; and take care of defects or omissions; and (2) To serve as a force leading the whole church constituency, and particularly the church organizations, into a clear comprehension of what the Christian education program should be and do. In such functions there is no place for bungling ignorance. There is however a very important place for keen comprehension and resolute, patient determination to see righteousness come to pass.

Further consideration of this matter will be found in Chapter VIII.

IV

THE GENERAL SUPERINTENDENT OR DIRECTOR

When anyone speaks of the Christian educational work of the church the average non-discriminating person probably thinks of the Sunday church school. That is not quite correct. Practically every organization and function of the church is in some respect educational. Missionary societies teach certain elements of Christian belief and conduct. Scout Troops or boys' or girls' clubs teach other elements. Social and recreational organizations, young people's and children's organizations of whatever description, even the official boards of the church, are all educational in their work. The board of trustees, for example, may be thought of as a purely administrative body in the realm of finance; yet everything done by this board has a strong influence in teaching good or bad habits with regard to proportionate giving—good or bad management of the resources of the church. In short, no aspect of the church program is without educational significance. In view of this fact the person who is to be an effective supervisor of the educational work of the local church must ultimately take upon himself a general responsibility for all the work.

Throughout these studies the point of view is that normally the pastor himself will have to assume this rôle. Ideally he will do it in an unofficial and advisory way, that will get things done with the least possible credit to himself and the greatest possible credit to others. But in a work so large as he has on his hands, with responsibilities reaching in every direction, he will certainly need a right-hand man to whom he may delegate as much as possible of the educational administration.

In most churches this right-hand man is the general superintendent of the Sunday church school. In a few he is a volunteer or paid director of Christian education. The general superintendent is rarely understood to have under his supervision more than the force and functioning of the Sunday church school, all other groups having their separate leaders, answerable to the pastor or church officials. For the present this type of organization will probably have to be tolerated; but as soon as possible the educational ministry of the church and its affiliated organizations must be understood as one; and in churches of more than three hundred members (or even in churches of any size) the pastor's right-hand man in Christian education, whether a paid or a volunteer worker, will be understood as having supervision of the entire educational work of the church; taking his lead, of course, from his own "chief," the pastor; and having his staff and board of Christian education to cooperate with him.

There are those who object to the suggestion that the Sunday church school should be the organization about which to gather and finally develop the entire educational work of the church. Their reason is twofold: (1) They feel that the average general superintendent does not have either the time properly to lead, or the understanding of the whole field of Christian education to make him able to lead, though he might have the time. They therefore feel that such a suggestion places too much power in the hands of one man and the organization which he builds. Our answer to this is that there is probably much to be said in that direction. Most superintendents are *not* ready for so great a responsibility. On the other hand, we would insist that very few men are any better fitted to lead a board of deacons as it should be led, or to lead a board of trustees in the management of the church's finances. We should also point out the fact that the reason for this present course of lessons is, a conviction on the part of many of us that the average pastor is not proving himself wholly equal to the great task of Christian educational leadership. Speaking out of our own observation, and in view of the difficulties of leadership all along the line, we should hesitate before becoming too dogmatic in discounting the capabilities of carefully selected laymen if they are guided over a period of probation and then are kept in close fellowship with the pastor, who it is assumed (assumed, mark you!) does actually know the work. (2) The second reason for being suspicious of putting central power in the hands of the Sunday church school is that in the school organization there is often a tendency to be too independent of the church and too unconscious of the fact that the school is really *under,* and not parallel with the church—that, to use an old and homely figure, the tail may wag the dog instead of the dog wagging the tail. If the school is thus in a position of competition with the church, then there should be an effort to establish a right understanding as to what the relationship really is. A fundamental misconception exists regarding the place of the church and the place of the school. The school should be somehow actually and organically a servant of the church. This is absolutely fundamental. "A house divided against itself can not stand."

The only reason as elsewhere indicated, why departmentalization of the whole educational work of the church is suggested, using the departmental staffs of the Sunday church school as a common nucleus for an extending supervision, is that here we already have together the greatest number of the people involved. The natural approach for the pastor in all his work *is to begin with the people.* Such problems of coordination as do develop in many local churches will have to be handled by the board of Christian education—of which more is said in Chapter VIII.

1. A Real Partnership

There is little point in discussing whether a paid director of Christian education is preferable to a volunteer director or a general superintendent. The difficulty of securing funds will usually have given the matter a practical settlement. The money question for the moment having been set aside, however, it ought to be said dogmatically that the answer to this question depends wholly upon the situation—by which one means to include the type of church, the type of pastor, the type of laymen available—and the type of director available. Money alone can never buy an effective Christian education program. There have been cases in which an intelligent layman has made, in terms of service, a contribution to the life of the church which could not readily be duplicated even though a generous salary were available; and then again, there have been cases in which the program seemed permanently blocked unless a well-selected, full-time, paid director could be imported.

Whoever this strategic person is to be, the relationship between him and the pastor ought to be very close. The two should understand and trust each other. They should be frank, humble, studious, and cooperative in their fellowship. If their relationship is not so characterized, something goes out of the educational life of the church.

2. A Good Pastor

If there does not seem to be the right relationship between the two, the pastor will observe the Scriptural injunction and first examine *himself*. It is surprising how frequently he will have to go no further for great fields of conquest. " First pluck the beam out of thine own eye, and then shalt thou see clearly to pluck the mote out of thy brother's eye."

On many points he may well test himself. Among others the following will in this connection be pertinent:

1. Does he really know the educational work well enough to make him worthy of being looked up to by his Sunday church school superintendent?

2. Is his "poise" such as to invite respect?

3. Is he possessed of a truly Christian spirit—does he actually live out the character qualities which he is trying to teach? Is he forgiving, or does he hold grudges? Is he humble and able to learn from other people, as he would like them to learn from him? In particular, can he learn from the superintendent and appreciate superior qualities which he may find in him? Is it pleasant to be with him, or is it a bore?

4. Is he free from jealousy because of the recognition which teachers and others properly give the superintendent?

5. Is he constructive in his suggestions? Can he put his thoughts in a lucid form so that they are at once understood?

6. Does he know the difference between driving and winning, and does he major in the latter?

7. Does he know how to wait when waiting is wisest, and to push when pushing is best?

8. Does he have good sense? Is he skilful in dealing with people?

If his score is good on all or most of these points, he will have little difficulty in getting along well with his superintendent or director. He will be able to maintain as much leadership as is needful and to cultivate a relationship of continuing growth.

3. A Good Superintendent

The writer's experience with superintendents has been very happy. The one with whom he is at present associated brings to his work a fulness of devotion, a keenness of ability, a thoroughness of method, a breadth of view and an elevation of Christian spirit that are unusual. When a minister is permitted so rare an association in Kingdom service he would be faulty in spiritual sensibility if he did not take occasion to register his abiding gratitude unto God. Yet as plans were being set up for these lessons, a ministerial friend, whose experience has been nothing like so happy, called attention to several cases quite as unusual in the opposite direction; insisting that these unhappy situations are common enough to require consideration in a study of this kind. First, however, let us describe a happy relationship.

The good general superintendent is a layman of strong native ability, such as would mark him for important responsibilities in the industrial, commercial, or professional world. Yet he has an unquestionable personal Christian experience, and from day to day is trying to cultivate a closer walk with Christ, just as he would expect his pastor to do. He takes the journals of Christian education, reads books and reviews of books in the field of his work; and avails himself of frequent opportunities to attend conventions and conferences that will broaden and enrich his comprehension. In order to do these things and many others he gives up many social pleasures, harmless, but that consume time which is necessary for study and planning in matters pertaining to his Christian service. Again and again the light from his den is seen burning late as he makes himself authoritative as a superintendent. When invitations multiply to engage himself with various board and committee tasks of a scattering character, he budgets his time and strength, giving up all but the most important things, and always having a clear understanding with himself and everyone else that his local church has a rightful claim upon the lion's share of the time he can devote to Christian service.

He carefully plans his work, recording what has been done and what has not been done, after the manner of a docket. He studies these records, and the reports of the school. He keeps familiar with what is happening all through its departments. To the most significant points he draws the attention of the pastor, with whom he frequently enters into conference. There is a full understanding between himself and his pastor that the general superintendent is the head of the school and at no time needs to await word from the pastor before acting upon any usual matter; yet in all questions of importance the two are so close to each other that they habitually talk things over, and find themselves greatly helped thereby. They are friends. They enjoy each other's company. Yet they are conscious of the fact that this same friendly relationship should be fostered throughout the entire official inner circle, and so they do all they can toward that end. The superintendent conducts the administrative meetings of the school, and is the leading spokesman on these occasions, but he sees to it that the pastor is near-by and readily available if an occasion of need arises. The two constantly confer on matters of personnel; and cooperate closely in the whole church program. There is no conflict but rather a mutually helpful relationship.

But what can be said of those cases in which the pastor and superintendent apparently can not work together? A problem of this kind is indeed serious. Fortunately, it does not frequently occur. But when it does, while patience is a great virtue, and love, long-suffering and kind, should prevail, yet the Christian teaching program of a church is too important to suffer at the hands of a selfish or non-cooperative person. The difficulty often is that the same qualities that make a superintendent undesirable make him also an influence of strength in the church. It is one thing to say he should be displaced, another to displace him. If there is a flagrant defect in moral conduct the evidence for which is beyond possible challenge, then of course quiet, courageous action should be prompt—the official board of the church acting in regular manner. If, however, it is the more common sort of thing that the superintendent is a misfit, the procedure is not so evident.

In the handling of most such problems the pastor will find it is rarely wise to act in haste, or to act without the backing of some official group. Usually he will want to be fairly sure he knows where he stands before he ventures far. Few pastors can permanently succeed in any church unless they have the backing of a majority of their official groups, and their official groups make it absolutely clear that they are ready to give this backing. In the average church it would very likely at once precipitate a crisis if the question of the superintendency were raised in a meeting of the board of deacons or trustees, because there would be friends of the superintendent who would say: "Just what business have the deacons or trustees meddling with the church school?" The atmosphere would quickly become surcharged with conflict. Worse things than this could happen, for as a matter of fact the board of deacons rightly does have all the business in the world "meddling" with any aspect of the church work that pertains to its spiritual life and influence. Still, a much more logical and less violent course could be followed if there were a regularly authorized Christian education board, having the necessary powers and responsibilities; a small group with whom the pastor can talk first individually and then collectively. If they feel the necessity of adjustment, the adjustment can very likely be managed, especially if the general superintendent is elected by the church. If they do not see its necessity, the pastor may accomplish more by turning back to the slow task of educating the inner circle in *the underlying principles of Christian work.* Forceful action is always to be avoided as long as possible. It cannot always be avoided. The perennial basis of all appeals in church work is *the righteousness* of the appeal—the manner in which each individual soul and the spiritual life of the entire church will be helped. This being the case, there have been instances in which individuals who seemed utterly hopeless have responded in sportsmanlike manner to a quiet, frank, personal conversation concerning the standards which the work should have and the manner in which these standards are to be achieved. An impersonal but continual holding up of clear and reasonable needs will often serve as a sifting means and obviate personal elements. It is better, though it may seem to be slower. The slow method is often, finally, the quickest and best.

These last two paragraphs have been reluctantly inserted simply because in some churches from fifty to seventy-five per cent. of that which is presented in these lessons is absolutely blocked by an individual person. Neither a pastor nor a superintendent need be a very unusual person, but if either of them is a stumbling-block in the way of the church—the church is more important than the person. To suffer long and to be kind is Scriptural; but just as mandatory is the injunction to lovingly speak the truth; or—in another connection—to see that justice rolls down like a mighty stream. "And what doth the Lord require of thee, but to do justly, and love kindness and to walk humbly with thy God?"

4. A Good Director

Professional directors of Christian education, during the first stage of their common acceptance—the past twenty-five years—have not proven so successful as it was expected they would be. Several reasons for this are to be found: (1) The task of Christian education is insistent, and it was somehow felt that miracles in this field would speedily be wrought if only a specialist, with a promissory name, were paid to accomplish them. That was too much to expect. (2) Often the director was loaded up with stenographic and secretarial duties, or with calling and other pastoral work that had only a remote connection with the educational program; and yet minister and people expected educational miracles to be achieved. (3) In numerous cases the pastor and director did not know how to work together in the educational program. Sometimes this was the fault of the pastor, sometimes of the director, often of both.

Underlying this course of lessons is the assumption that the pastor, ordinarily, has to be the head of Christian education as he is the head of all other work of the church. The director is directed by the pastor, and is strongly backed by the pastor. His work is given a dignity in the church that makes him approach people with a full confidence on his part and on theirs. The director is simply a part of the pastor, each sympathizing with the other so completely and understanding the whole church task so fully that they work as one person. There should never be an uncertainty as to who is the head. It should, beyond question, be the pastor. If he is unfit, then the whole administration goes by the board; but unless the defects of the pastor are so outstanding as to lead the church in a regular way to declare him incompetent there should not be a moment's hesitation as to where full leadership authority resides. A secretary, or director, or other assistant, should be selected largely on the pastor's word and should be accountable directly to the pastor and his Board of Christian Education. From the very beginning this allocation of authority should be clearly understood. In other words, a pastor should have as much authority over his paid staff as a business executive has over his force. There is no other sensible procedure.

If this obvious and basic principle is understood the way is clear for an organization to be built up without having each one in the staff working according to his own ideas and interests. A policy can be outlined with clear-cut plans. It may be that it is needful for a director in a particular situation to give mornings to secretarial work, early afternoons to study and program-planning, and later afternoons and evenings to special calling, teaching, conference, dramatization and recreation work. If he feels that secretarial work is unprofessional, let him be consoled with the knowledge that the great majority of pastors—even the best of them—are constantly giving large blocks of their time to exactly this sort of thing. The position is not for him unless he is willing to do the things that have to be done. But if both pastor and director are driven by a high purpose of service, if they study the work and divide it and really help each other, then a great and increasing thrill awaits them at every turn in the road.

This having been said, it should be added that in cases where pastor-and-director combinations have failed the responsibility for such failure should be placed on the pastor fully as much as on the director. By advising, helping and strongly backing the director, the pastor's own program can be greatly advanced; as he can thus relieve himself of many burdens. The director, however, can rarely do well at his job without the pastor's cooperation and sympathy.

5. The Church's Part

The general fellowship of the church also has a large influence in determining what either a professional director or a volunteer general superintendent can do. No matter how much either of these may give in time and ability, the effectiveness of his service can be well-nigh nullified if the entire congregation does not realize that all must be united in the task. The best of workers become discouraged with the hindrances and unpleasantnesses that thoughtless people put in their way. Especially is the volunteer superintendent tempted to say to himself: "I am a volunteer and do not have to suffer criticism and make constant sacrifice simply in order to do work that is just as much the duty of all these other people as it is mine. If they appreciated it I might feel differently; but they do not see the value it has to their children." Many have fallen by the wayside because there was no redress for the unjust punishments they had endured from thoughtless people in the church fellowship. To be sure, they ought not thus to "weaken," but the temptation is constantly there, and people are human.

If in place of either sitting back and waiting for the superintendent or director to somehow get the work done, all the congregation would build the attitude of appreciation and encouragement—the pastor of course leading—it would often be the means of actually *making* a great superintendent or director. He may be courageous. He may not be the kind who cares for recognition. Flattery may be embarrassing and distasteful to him; but there is a deep and earnest sort of appreciation that has none of the cheapness of flattery's voice. The church will do well to cultivate it.

V

THE PASTOR AND THE DEPARTMENTAL SUPERINTENDENT

The pastor and the general superintendent were seated on opposite sides of a table in the church parlor. A third chair was unoccupied. It was evident they were expecting someone. Presently she arrived.

"Good evening, Miss Jones," said the two men as they rose and motioned her to the place at the end of the table. After a few moments of informal conversation the superintendent began:

"We certainly appreciate your giving us this time tonight, and yet we are convinced you are as deeply interested as we in the work about which we wish to confer. You are familiar with the fact that for some weeks our primary department has been without an active superintendent, and it is because we should like you to take the leadership of this group that we have asked you here tonight."

Miss Jones is being faced with a serious question. Her ability to lead, her spiritual life, her willingness to sacrifice many social contacts that may be pleasant, her health, perhaps her daily employment—all these things and many others come into her mind and halt her progress toward an affirmative answer.

It is not easy for her to sacrifice the things she knows she must if she is properly to do this service But the trouble is, there are other consequences if she does not. The pastor and superintendent point out to her some of them, the latter for a few moments acting as spokesman.

1. "Bad Religion Is Being Ably Taught Today"

"No one seriously concerned about our boys and girls will dare to disregard four facts:

(1) The serious influence of the moving-pictures being exhibited on our screens.
(2) The danger presented by the liquor traffic.
(3) The devastating effects of war talk and war influences.
(4) The serious fact that large numbers of parents and other adults are setting an example that is, at best, bewildering to children and youth, and, at worst, degrading.

"It would be instructive for us to discuss at length each of these. They are terrific factors. Other matters, however, just now press for attention. We shall have to trust you to fill in the details. In fair measure we believe you recognize the significance of each.

"On the first point, however, we should like to say a word before we go on, especially in view of its very timely character. It will serve to illustrate the sort of facts which are pertinent to each of the four points:

"The nine large scientific studies of the various aspects of the motion-picture industry have now been ably summarized and evaluated in a volume by Henry James Forman. The case against the industry is overwhelming. Seventy-seven million weekly attendants at the motion-picture theatres is the conservative number. Of these, twenty-eight million are under twenty-one years of age and the bulk of them are unattended by adults. Eleven million are thirteen years or under.

"Out of a random sampling of fifteen hundred pictures carefully studied it was found there was a great overloading of crime and indecent suggestion.

"Even the youngest attendants, it was discovered, carried away with them between 50 per cent. and 70 per cent. of what they saw; and the strange thing about it is that after the passage of some time they remembered more rather than less. The carefully detailed scientific investigations from which these general truths are established leave no doubt as to their soundness. Thoroughly trustworthy means were employed to determine the good or bad effects of movies upon sleep, nerves, criminal inclinations, moral conduct and the like. The case against the industry is quite established.

" When we realize how much more can be said about this factor, and about each of the other three, we begin to understand we are facing terrific odds in our attempts at Christian education.

" How can the church give to boys and girls influenced by such factors the best possible chance for the life that is the light of men? Taking the whole matter by and large, we shall have to admit that the church is only partly measuring up to its duty. The call is urgent, first of all to parents—that they will bear their rightful responsibility, not trying to shift it to the church.

" They can not properly pass this burden to others. It is *their* part to understand that the church is all but helpless unless their example, their teaching, their conversation and conduct lead boys and girls on in ways of righteousness.

" In spite of all that has been said about youth disregarding the teachings of adults, parental example is of tremendous power. The church cannot take over this province of parenthood. The best it can do is to aid the home. How? That is what we are tonight asking you to answer."

2. The Departmental Superintendent Is Strategic

" The large school, you have observed, Miss Jones, is a group of small schools closely working together. Departments are teaching-fellowships that have to develop a consciousness of their own, though always fully cooperating with each other. It can immediately be seen then how vastly important is the work of the leaders. The departmental superintendent is put in her position with the understanding that her responsibility goes in two directions:

"(1) *To the department itself,* inside closed doors, so to speak; the actual educative process under her leadership coming right down to each child.

"(2) *To the school and church as a whole,* relating the work of the department to these larger sponsoring organisms through the executive committee; and, in the opposite direction, relating the work of the school as a whole to the department."

There was a brief pause, and then a number of informal questions and answers growing out of the developing topic, after which the pastor with evident emotion said:

"I personally feel that our church school is quite favored in having Mr. Barrett as its general superintendent. I have no hesitation in saying to him, or to you, or to the church that I regard him as our minister of Christian education. Very properly he stands out as one of God's marked men, ordained to a particular sort of ministry. I think of him as second in command. To him it is necessary to delegate the bulk of the responsibility for the administration of the school.

"But, the better he does his work as a volunteer minister of education, the more earnestly will he strive to stimulate and set free the powers of each departmental superintendent, so that he or she can become through the department a potent influence for Christ. The general superintendent understands this. The pastor understands it. They know full well that a task so great has to be divided, in order that it may be concentrated upon. The departmental superintendent is the answer."

Again the general superintendent took up the conversation:

"By this, however, the pastor does not in any sense mean to decrease our estimate of the teacher's task. The teacher is the agent through whom much of the work must be done; but, after all, the departmental superintendent is the one who must constantly find the proper teachers and lead them in doing their work."

With quiet and earnest conversational manner, question and answer freely passing from one to another, the concerns and needs of one who was to do this work were then taken up. A summary of the thought presented in this case chiefly by the superintendent, the pastor supplementing freely, is something as follows:

3. Some Concerns of the Departmental Superintendent

(1) *She*[1] *has the responsibility for the worship programs in her department.* To plan and direct this, whether she actually leads in it or has someone else lead, is an every week concern. Materials, conferences, plans and work are constantly necessary. Though the pastor need not always and cannot always be in these conferences—in fact there are many occasions when it is well for him not to be present—he will always be watching for materials to place in the departmental superintendent's hands. He will try to give her helpful suggestions, choosing the right time and the right manner.

(2) *The matter of improving teaching by supervision is one of her very great concerns.* It is, in some cases, a delicate point. She will want to be able to observe and make suggestions to the teachers—not in a critical, but in a truth-seeking spirit. Sometimes she will be able to do this better if she goes into the classes and studies the teachers' methods. Teachers can help her by making her feel easy about such a practice. She

[1] Out of deference to Miss Jones the feminine pronoun is here used—with no suggestion, however, that a departmental superintendent should be a woman.

is there as a friendly helper. She is interested in the boys and girls and wants to do for them the very best possible. The pastor will help in preparing for this more natural and congenial visitation and supervision by spreading abroad, both in the congregation and with the teachers individually and collectively, the expectation of congenial helpfulness. He can make to the group as a whole suggestions which, if made to individuals, might sometimes not be so readily accepted. And in a hundred ways he will further the work of supervision by and with her.

(3) *She has the management of the department.* Departmental conferences are times when she hopes and prays that the work may be raised to a higher level. It is not easy either to plan or to conduct these occasions. She hopes for a generous, unselfish, loyal response. Often she gets it. Sometimes she does not. It depends in fair measure on her program. The pastor and general superintendent will be watching for helpful suggestions and materials for conference conduct. New materials will be handed to her, and she will come to feel that suggestions are to be expected. The friendly relations between herself, the general superintendent and the pastor will be fruitful of many a step forward. In all this the general superintendent and the pastor will be in the closest partnership. The former is the executive head of the school; the latter the fatherly adviser and leader of all branches of the church and school. As much as possible he delegates of course to others, but he is back of it all.

(4) *The esprit de corps of the department is her constant anxiety.* Nothing can more harmfully wear upon one who is possessed of a high and noble soul than to feel elements of selfishness, jealousy, *sin,* pulling down the spirit of the department and eating out its deeper life. Children sense the existence of these poisonous things far more quickly than adults realize.

They do not understand the cause nor do they know the exact character of what is happening, but they do quickly feel an unwholesome relationship, or an unwholesome spirit, on the part of those who are supposed to lead them into better things. It is obviously a subject of prayer on the part of the pastor, the general superintendent and the departmental superintendent, that as largely as possible such things may be kept out of the life of the group.

If difficulties arise, as they surely will, and the departmental superintendent needs help, she will first go to the general superintendent. If he is of the right spirit he will usually be able to iron out the difficulties as helpfully as the pastor could, or even more so. It will be understood that usually such procedure is best. Though at certain times the pastor must assume the hazardous rôle of arbitrator, or judge, and though at such times he must be courageous, kindly and cool, he must not forget that his position as shepherd of the entire flock will be strengthened rather than weakened by bringing about the needed adjustments through the work of the department leader herself or the general superintendent. Especially matters which have to do with personal animosities, jealousies, and the like, can have very detrimental effect on the public's attitude toward the pastor—if he gets into them unnecessarily. At times he may have to; but whenever it is reasonably possible he should be protected from the flight of the poisoned arrows of bickering and irritation. Very likely if he stays in the background he will soon have opportunity to exert an even greater influence; for the first effort at downing these evil spirits may not prove effective. A discreet pastoral call in the homes disturbed by the adjustment may be the means of saving the church from injury that, but for the call, might ensue. He is then present in the rôle of a true shepherd and not that of an executive or judge. It will require all the wisdom, gentleness and honesty he can bring to bear upon people. Diplomacy, a very valuable and necessary attribute of the pastor, has often degenerated into duplicity. In this busy age it is sometimes felt by Christian workers that people have outgrown the ministry of pastoral home prayer in effecting harmony and real devotion to the cause of Christ. They have not. To be sure there are some for whom prayer is like a foreign language of which they know a few words only, the rest being too strange for every-day use. A minister who presumed to pray with them would immediately be adjudged sanctimonious, or "not practical enough." That such an attitude exists is in part our own fault. We have been either remiss in training people, or unreal in our own spiritual habits. The present writer is deeply convinced that pastoral prayer in the home, particularly in dealing with special problems or burdens, should be engaged in more frequently.

It is fairly safe to say that if a person becomes involved in a tangle of personal animosities and then will not regard as appropriate a sincere experience of prayer which has been suggested and prepared for by his pastor (if that pastor's own devotional life and moral example ring true), it is extremely unlikely that the person in question can be of present use in a Christian educational program. Prayer is at the center of the Christian religion, and he who has no vital prayer experience, or who does not respond to such an experience, is attempting to give others that which he does not himself possess. Frankness, in such a case is best; not Phariseeism, but the humblest and most earnest sort of frankness. The supreme ministry of the pastor as a diplomat is, therefore, a deeply spiritual one. Perhaps he can save a worker for the department (or school); certainly he must save the *spirit of the school.*

The departmental superintendent will always go as far as possible in this direction. It is assumed that she herself is thoroughly imbued with the Spirit. Yet it must be remembered that she is a volunteer worker. She is constantly with these people in the department. In putting forward the normally needed plans she may at times come upon difficulties in which she needs the help of one who is especially set apart for the sort of spiritual guidance above suggested. At that point the pastor will be prompt and careful.

(5) *She is also a sort of "under-pastor."* She is concerned about the spiritual and material welfare of all in the department, both pupils and leaders. She is trying to bring these persons through a growing Christian experience. In that experience all the unusual events of life have an important function. Death, for example, comes into a home. The departmental superintendent will not miss hearing the call at such a time to be a sympathizing friend. If she is first to get word of the events, she will immediately tell teacher and pastor. Careful to make their calls serve the best needs, and as many needs as possible, they will work together according to a well-considered plan that has grown out of a study of the needs. God is very near when the angel of death passes by. He must be understood by the child, the youth, the adult. People who would bring comfort can easily talk too much, though they mean well; but they cannot sympathize too deeply if their sympathy is real. The pastor will therefore help to teach by example and skilful suggestion how teacher and superintendent can be most helpful—and incidentally he may also profit by taking suggestions from superintendent and teacher as together they go with the family through the hard experience.

In like manner there will come times of unusual poverty; times of anxiety about some difficult life-problem; times of joy over some happy event; a graduation, a marriage, a promotion, an anniversary, a new baby. The pastor, if he is alive to the situation, understands that these times offer opportunity for a fuller interpretation of Christian faith and life. So he and the departmental superintendent will use strategy in planning how they may be the best sort of Christian leaders for the persons involved. Experience will lead the pastor to believe it is needful to regard the department superintendent as the key-person in seeing that this sort of thing is attended to. The teacher, to be sure, is closest to the pupil; but the department superintendent is the one who will always be responsible for seeing that somehow the matter is attended to by someone. Of course the pastor will be prompt with his ministries, but there will be many details. Upon these the departmental superintendent will "check," to see that they really are done.

She will help him with the more definitely evangelistic aspects of the work, preparing the way through worship programs and departmental atmosphere, and bringing boys and girls, men and women, face to face with the great life decision, for a Yes or No answer at the appropriate season. She will follow the church relationship of those in her department, calling the pastor's and the teacher's attention to a growing or diminishing interest on the part of any member of the department. She will want to know about their attendance at the church services; participation in the work program of the church, and in the witnessing aspect of the Christian life. In other words she is exactly what was suggested above, an under-pastor of her department.

Personal evangelism, naturally but earnestly conducted, is an extremely important thing. If teachers, departmental superintendents, general superintendent, pastor, parents, all concerned, are in the right frame of mind—"in tune with the Spirit"—the work moves forward with wholesome and generous results; but if they are not in such frame of mind, not in tune with the Spirit, the work is likely to be chilled and stunted.

The conduct of a wise evangelism is not to be thought of as like the manufacture or sale of inanimate merchandise, though we do too frequently so think of it. It is much more like the growing of choice roses—a process in which the most skilful nurturing is required, and in which the condition of the surrounding atmosphere must be carefully regarded. The honest friendliness, the wholesomeness of life, the warm, pulsating, Christian example, of these older companions is of infinite worth. The departmental superintendent will be carefully regardful of this fact.

(6) There is another important task; to introduce those in her department to the pastor. It is of course his place to be attentive to this matter. Still the departmental superintendent must look out for it. If one considers the little children, for example, he will be quite surprised to learn how frequently the pastor is quite a "foreigner" to the thinking and life of many of them. The older ones should be with their parents in the family pew; but they are not always found there. It is needful that the pastor should be an expected visitor at the children's affairs, the schedule of his arrival and departure being such that he will not interrupt, but rather share in the departmental experiences and contribute something to the children's enjoyment and benefit. So far as possible he should know the children by name, or at least by family connection, making the matter of such acquaintance a really serious part of his pastorate. In many churches it is assumed that the minister's wife should be president of the woman's society. There is good reason for believing, however, that she can be of greater use when active in some phase of the children's work, where she will enable her husband to keep in close relationship with the children and their homes. As he goes through the various departments of the school each Sunday morning his friendly greetings to individual boys and girls and their

leaders will build a better pastoral relationship with this important part of his parish.

4. The Type

It is obvious that such an assistant to the pastor as the departmental superintendent is to be, must be a person of high type. She is " a headquarters officer "—in rank only the second step from the pastor. Without fair native ability she will be sure to have hard going, for much has to be expected of her. She is a volunteer, and may be inclined to remember this when she feels the injustice of some crosses she has to bear. Without saying too much, the pastor, at these times, will encourage her by sharing with her the interpretation of the Master's experiences, which clearly indicate that the servant must expect some of the Master's anguish, perhaps pointing out to her that these things come to everyone—even a pastor—and that true followers of Christ must carry such burdens in such a way as to learn to grow, not groan, under them. He will try to inspire her even to the point of getting a bit of a thrill out of the sense that she is exemplifying the love that suffereth long and is kind, that taketh no account of evil, and that never faileth. Her way, like his, often passing through Gethsemane, will also pass over mountains of joy and by rivers of quietness; the city to which it will ultimately come will be the City of God; and with her there will be a great rejoicing throng, in the making of whose lives she has had a part.

VI

GROWING LEADERS TO MEET GOD'S GRADING

There are still plenty of churches in which an argument can be started on the question of *the Graded* versus *the Uniform Lessons.* In defense of the latter it can truthfully be said that there is a vigorous appeal in having all ages and groups at one time studying the same subject-matter. No uncertainty need prevail as to what the lesson is to be. It was in the newspaper yesterday; if the paper is not lost you can go and read it this very minute.

1. People Are Graded

But whether *the Uniform* or *the Graded* Lessons are used, a lesson that is well taught is always graded to the age making up the class. In other words, God graded the children when he created them, and no matter what man may do to the contrary, they still are graded. The five-year-old is utterly different from the nine-year-old; the nine-year-old, from the fourteen-year-old; the fourteen-year-old, from the nineteen-year-old; and the nineteen-year-old, from the thirty-year-old. The facts of creation are not changed by man's failure to observe them. It is therefore not merely a question of what lessons shall be used; rather of what kind of persons are to be taught. Graded lessons merely recognize that there is this year-by-year change in the characteristics of children and young people, and that it is wise to prepare for each age group the nearest possible approach to a-lesson-suited-to-the-interests.

The difficulties encountered in carrying out with exact precision this ideal are twofold: (1) Though the growing child is each year different from the year before, the various children of a given age are also different *from each other.* They have not started at any given age from exactly the same mark, nor have they advanced with equal pace. Like a flock of sheep moving leisurely across a pasture, at one time some are ahead, at another, others; yet they keep leisurely moving in this irregular formation and finally reach the other side of the field, as a flock. (2) Though age characteristics are known to exist, though there can be little questioning of the fact that God has graded the children, the second difficulty is correctly to list the age-group characteristics and then select and arrange lesson materials that will suit the needs.

This, however, is a field by itself. As so much thorough attention already has been given to it, discussion here is superfluous. If the student wishes to refresh his memory on the subject let him turn to any standard leadership training text dealing with the pupil and the teacher; or let him run through the various books dealing with departmental methods. For the present we are simply assuming that there are fairly defined group characteristics, now pretty well known, following these years:

Nursery—under 4 (Nursery Class 3 years old).
Beginners—4 and 5.
Primary—6 to 8 inclusive.
Junior—9 to 11 inclusive.
Intermediate—12 to 14 inclusive.
Senior—15 to 17 inclusive.
Young People—18 to 24 inclusive.
Adults—25 and up.
Home Department—all who cannot attend the school sessions—any age.

The adult group may be further divided into young adults (25 to 40) and older adults (41 plus); or it may be divided along the lines of *kinds-of-interest.* For the present purpose the more general age grouping will serve. What one wishes to do is not merely to hold to some arbitrary grading, but rather to approach as nearly as possible the absolute facts of human nature and wholesome Christian experience.

This, then, is what the pastor has to begin with as he turns his attention to the problem of developing personnel for the local church program of Christian education. They are more or less distinct groups and each of them requires a leader with special knowledge and aptitudes concerning that particular group. How shall these leaders be furnished?

2. Discovering Leaders

The pastor should always be on the search for prospective teachers and leaders. In his own file or in the file of his superintendent—or in both—there might well be a folder labeled "Personnel." If he uses the loose-leaf note-book, keeping all his thoughts and plans of an educational character under one cover, he may keep the data there. But wherever he has it and by whatever system he cultivates it, an annotated list of names is helpful. If the church is not large he may feel that writing the names is needless; that he can recall the right one at the right time; but with most men this is not a correct assumption. There are times when needs develop quickly. Some of the very best prospects are not immediately thought of because they are on the edges of the fellowship. The result is that the pastor names, or allows a nominating committee to name, a person who already has from one to three tasks, and so has to be loaded too heavily, or removed from one of the positions already held.

But if the pastor has an annotated list, he can run rapidly over it, in the presence of the committee seeking advice, calling attention, of course, only to those fitted for the work in question. The fact that he has here a list of some about whom he has been thinking as possible children's leaders, for example, will have led him to give them suggestions and advice looking in that direction, so they will be partly ready. Similarly with those of whom he is thinking in connection with young people's or adult work. He may even have had a casual conversation with them about it. Very likely at the time they will have said, "Oh, no! I could not do a thing like that"; but if he has properly called attention to the ever-recurring need, and has revealed the plan of looking for prospective leaders, and has refused to take an easy No for an answer, there will be a tendency on the part of the prospect to prepare as much as possible, "lest a call might come."

Promises of work will not be made definite except where there is a strong conviction the prospect really is suitable—that is, has the qualities that will develop into suitableness. The idea can be sown as a seed, without setting the time or designating the manner of harvesting.

At any rate the pastor will constantly be on the lookout for leaders of every description. *He will make it a major matter in his work.* He will be in frequent conference with his superintendent, leaving many matters of final placement to him; but, because of the pastor's greater opportunity to know people through home visitation, he will be able greatly to assist the superintendent. Sometimes people will have to be injected into positions for which they have had little special training. There is no one more nearly ready than they, and so they must go on as best they can, studying the work while they are right at it. The pastor in these cases will be conscious of their need of help, and without smothering or crushing them all at once with an avalanche of literature and suggestions, will say the right thing and furnish the right materials to foster growth. At least he will take pains to call in the home of the new worker, or otherwise to contact him, and in the spirit of real sympathetic interest ask how the new work is coming along; whether there is a feeling of getting hold upon it; and whether there is anything he can do to help.

Good leaders are far more plentiful than is commonly supposed. They have to be developed; and getting them started is the pastor's real problem. Many who say "I can't" are sincere. They really do not know how. They could learn, but they do not know how to go at it. No one has ever shown them. To continue in their present state of casual interest and inactivity is the most natural thing in the world. To change is a bother, and so they do not change. But if once they can get a taste of successful, unselfish leadership—can discover how to do the work and where to get materials for still greater improvement—they are caught in the meshes of the habit of leadership, with the same grip that any other habit has upon them. Their whole life is henceforth likely to follow a different course. The problem is to win people to a Christlike spirit of service, and then to get them started in the direction of doing the work increasingly well.

3. The Pastor and Leadership Training

The search for leaders and the giving of such scattered help as is above suggested, will not entirely suffice. There are certain basic principles which can just as well be taught to ten or twenty people as to one at a time. A leadership training department is therefore as essential as the other departments. All sorts of theories are advanced why the pastor should or should not teach in the Sunday school. Certain it is, that properly to teach a lesson in the hour immediately before the morning worship is too taxing on his nervous strength—which should be at a high mark at the time of his sermon. Of course this teaching would bring him close to the life of the people whom he teaches, and thus key him up to a more vital and living message. But whatever may be the conclusion on this point, experience leads one to say that there is no one who can quite take the place of the pastor as the teacher of frequent leadership training courses. He should not be reluctant about accepting the responsibility of being superintendent of the training department. Some of the courses may be taught by others who have been carefully selected, but a fair portion of them may well be handled by himself. The value of this is obvious. He has the opportunity of discussing first-hand all the general and many of the specialization points having to do with leadership throughout the church and school; quickening in the people who make up the class—especially the young people—a hunger to serve, by building in their minds a picture of how to serve and why. Nor should the fact be overlooked that it keeps fresh in the mind of the pastor himself correct principles and methods of Christian education. He is held close to the throbbing heart of the educational work of the whole church. As he teaches how things should be done, the natural tendency for himself and for members of the class is to ask, "Where is this principle to be seen in our own church? How are we ourselves measuring up on this point?" The result is a constant flow of suggestions for improvement in church and school.

Opportunities for special leadership courses at the Sunday school hour will be found in the following ways: (1) By using a ten or twelve lesson training course as an "elective" with a young people's class—not changing the class arrangement at all. (2) By making up a special young people's class, hand-picking the more promising and the more interested from any or all the classes. (3) By using either of these procedures in the adult department. (4) By constructing a mixed class made up of interested persons, regardless of age.

In any one of these cases thorough work is unlikely to be done without devoting more than twelve sessions to a course; particularly if the training class has only the usual half-hour, or less, which most Sunday schools devote to the lesson. If credit is desired—and this is to be recommended—there are certain minimum time and study requirements to be met. These are indicated in the leadership training circulars. Experience will probably lead one to concentrate upon a special class selected for a given period of time with the particular objective of completing one course. This will also be more fruitful if they understand that the course assumes that those taking it wish to prepare for work in the church or school.

In addition to the classes held at the Sunday school session there will be others arranged for some week-night; or before or after the Sunday evening worship; or in connection with the midweek service. In many communities it will also be possible to run a community training school, in which all the churches join together; thus sharing the best available instructors.

It will be noted that the classes held at the school hour have one serious limitation in that they do not permit those who are active in the teaching work to participate. There are two cures for this: (1) The provision of such other classes as are indicated in the last paragraph; and (2) the temporary release of certain teachers from their regular work in order that they may devote three or six months to the special study. The former of the two is probably the more feasible; the latter, though not so commonly used, has real possibilities.

The leadership training department—of which the pastor is presumably superintendent—finds one of its most important functions to be that of improving teaching by supervision. The pastor is not likely to be able personally to make regular visits upon all classes. Certainly he will not if he is majoring as a teacher of the leadership training class at the school hour. But he can gradually impress upon the various departmental superintendents the fact that supervision is the best method of training, since the student learns how to do the work while actually at the work itself. As a matter of fact supervision includes almost every possible form of guidance and instruction. The ideal method of training probably is for the student to take from one to four general courses and then plunge into work under competent supervision. After having gotten a start at this, it will be time to take up more advanced courses, meanwhile continuing in the active teaching work under close oversight.

Nothing will more effectively do the work of training for leadership than an organization that is made up of a high percentage of good leaders. It requires a long time to build this. Once it is well started, however, each succeeding step is more easily taken. A novice discovers that there are coming to him from every side suggestions for improvement, and that there is about him an atmosphere of expectation that improvement will be made. There is the feeling that anything that *ought* to be done *can* be done—indeed *must* be done. Supervision is taking place by at least half the people over themselves and all the rest; and yet none of them knows that anyone at all is supervising. The nurturing and perfecting of leadership here is merely a process of fruit-bearing; and it is the best imaginable mode of training. The fruit-grower who wishes an abundance of good apples gives attention to the size, color, shape and taste of individual fruit; but before long he learns that after all the way to get good apples is to raise *good apple trees.* These, properly selected to begin with, and then constantly pruned, nurtured and guarded from blight and insect, bear year after year a plentiful harvest. Care is the constant requirement. That is the fruit-grower's task.

Such is the highest leadership training function of the pastor. He uses his whole organization as a place in which to grow leaders. Though people of ability who are injected into the primary department will be fashioned by that particular department until their abilities are bent in the direction of the children who are there, and though in the junior or intermediate or kindergarten departments the same will prevail, a teaching process in leadership will thus be carried forward more powerfully than by any other means he might devise. His most economical method, therefore, of training leaders will be so to stimulate these departments and the whole organization as to fit them constantly to bear the fruit of trained leadership.

VII

EQUIPMENT IS STUBBORN

The pastor will feel a personal responsibility for the provision of the best possible building and equipment. No matter how good the text-books, or how skilled the teachers, it can all be negated by handicaps in the way of surroundings. Who would place a class of junior boys in the front seats of a large circus and expect them to get the point of the Sunday school lesson when simultaneously trained animals were performing immediately before them, trick-riders were amazing the crowds to the left, a mock battle was being conducted by clowns to the right, and a triple flying-trapeze act was going forward in the top of the tent? To be sure, even in the most difficult of one-room schools the distractions are not quite so engaging as these; but the principle is the same, the difference being more in degree than in kind. The conditions which limit attention in secular education equally limit it in Christian education; and while it is unlikely the latter will ever be able to match the former in equipment, it is always well to know under what conditions the latter is working. If it can be improved even to a limited extent it is well to understand how important that slight improvement may be.

1. The Influence of a Building

A church determines the sort of building it will have; but the building has a large influence in determining what sort of church it will have. There is, to begin with, the general impression that a building makes. It has an atmosphere—a personality. At first sight it is either beautiful or ugly. It inspires or depresses. In its very shadow there seems to linger a glory or a gloom. It may be a good place for worship, but a poor place for study or play or work. Conversely, it may be a good place for study or play or work, but a poor place for worship.

If visitors find a plant that gives them the immediate impression that provision is being made for the child their enthusiasm rises. They return. Somehow they feel they would like to belong where the type of work is being done which this building advertises. On the other hand, if the immediate suggestion of the building is that little attention is paid to the Christian education of the young, a sudden cooling of interest takes place.

Or, let us suppose teachers and workers are being solicited and the building is good. Is there not greater likelihood that the response will be favorable: "You give teachers a chance by giving them tools with which to work! I shall be glad to try my hand."

Now, while this is not a sound basis upon which to win workers for Jesus Christ, capable teachers are not to be blamed if they consider such matters when they are deciding how they can best use their talents; and incidentally they are judging on a fairly sound basis when they conclude that, because we have poor equipment, we think less than we should of the importance of properly teaching growing lives the way of Christ. King David was perfectly right in being ashamed of himself for living as he did in a magnificent palace, while worshiping God in a dingy, stingy place that did nothing but proclaim how secondary divine worship really was at his court.

Even the pastor can be so burdened with the consciousness that his building is inadequate that he finally pities himself and settles down to the routine of "doing the best he can" under conditions that are very bad. He should never thus surrender; but he is human and so he sometimes does. When that happens it is a sad day indeed for the educational program of his church. On the other hand, if he has a good plant in which to work, how it thrills him! He is like a skilled mechanic with a splendid set of tools instead of a few of the clumsy home-made sort. His building and equipment are his tools.

2. The Pastor's Place in a New Building Decision

He cannot usually force the issue either of a new building enterprise or of substantial modification of present facilities. He is not a dictator, nor are his judgments "true and righteous altogether." He is the leader of his people, however, and can have almost a deciding influence in the issues of the church, if he is patient, wise and persistent.

He will do well to refresh and stimulate his mind with the story of Nehemiah, the great rebuilder of the walls of Jerusalem; for he must be more or less like that Old Testament worthy. As Nehemiah went out by night and skirted the city, prayerfully studying the strong and the broken places in the wall, no one looking on but the silent stars and "the eyes that look through," so the pastor must go into every corner of his building and study it in the quiet—alone. He must know every foot of floor and wall, and every window, and note their possibilities. And then he must go all through it again when the people are there. He must observe the locations, distractions, merits, possibilities of adaptation, places where trades could be made to advantage, and so on.

If a growing school and wholly inadequate facilities call beyond doubt for a major building operation, he will of course move slowly and carefully, realizing how salutary right action may now prove, but what utterly tragic results can follow in the path of a mistaken leadership. As the decisions all have to be finally made by the people, and the money expended must come from them, he will lead them in studying the problem, and assist them in getting all the pertinent data, in order that they may decide as fairly as possible in view of the knowable facts. Before he goes far he will quite likely wish privately to consult experienced outside advisers.

One successful venture, culminating in a large educational building, facing at its beginning practically all the problems of skepticism and poverty that such undertakings usually face, went forward by the following steps:

1. Throughout a period of years leaders had been developed in the Sunday church school for as many of the standard departments as possible; each gradually being imbued with the best ideals and methods in Christian education. Thus there came into existence all through the school groups of people who deeply felt the need of better equipment. They quietly but repeatedly told exactly how they were handicapped and what harm was being done by it.
2. The general superintendent and the pastor were finally agreed that the time was ripe for a thorough study of the question, resulting in whatever decision might seem wise. It was therefore recommended *to the school,* in this case (for they were the ones who most urgently felt the need), that the school raise during the coming year $1,000 to be used, all or in part, in carefully studying the problem and getting the best possible guidance. It was clearly understood this money was a price the people were willing to pay for expert guidance. It did not assume that a building was to be built. The needs of the school were surveyed, and probable gains calculated, by the general superintendent, in constant conference with the pastor. An architect, experienced in counseling with churches, was engaged, with a clear understanding as to what his capacity was, namely, advisory in a preliminary survey. A small committee, representative of the church, joined the general superintendent and pastor; visits were made to the best plants that could be found; floor plans of a possible building were prepared; the approximate figure of cost set; and everything put in form preparatory to a presentation of the question to the church.
3. The whole plan was set forth with drawings, approximate figures, reasons for the building, etc., in a neatly printed, illustrated booklet. Within the booklet was a formal proposal to the church, signed by the committee, and in essence recommending that the church undertake

the building enterprise, *if* there could be secured pledges amounting to at least 55 per cent. of the estimated cost; and that contracts should not be placed until at least $10,000 in cash had been received. At a general church meeting, following a church dinner, the whole proposal was made and described, and at the same time it was reported that the pastor and general superintendent had interviewed a few families including 37 members of the church, who had tentatively declared themselves willing to subscribe a total of $22,000. The total cost was estimated at $75,000. The decision was to launch the campaign to secure pledges for the full amount, and to go ahead, if the conditions as formerly stated were met.

4. When pledges were secured covering more than $65,000, the building committee was appointed and the work went forward.

Many details are of course omitted from the foregoing description. The whole movement consumed several years before the decision was submitted to the church. A pastor leading his church into such a thing might well examine all those details, which, in this case, were carried through without the importation of any professional help aside from the consulting architect. It is in these earlier steps, leading up to the submission of a plan to a church, that mistakes fatal to a building enterprise are often made. A pastor who expects in a few weeks time to catapult an entire people into a building enterprise is likely to be sadly disappointed; or to find himself in possession of a whole brood of problems for the solution of which his people, with some justice, will be apt to hold him accountable. The soil must always be carefully prepared for the sowing of the seed, in any enterprise. Pastors do not as a rule take sufficient account of this important truth.

3. Improving Equipment at Slight Expense

Far more common is the necessity of modifying old equipment, or of adapting that which is fairly good. This is by no means an ignoble function. Many a school, so situated that a new structure is quite out of the question, has notably improved its facilities by a wise expenditure of very limited means. A church, for example, in western Pennsylvania, largely by volunteer work and with the expenditure of an almost paltry sum, has made good use of formerly " dead " overhead space, and has adapted to splendid educational use the remainder of the entire building—which might have been considered rather hopeless educationally. For the past fifteen years they have had a fairly modern home-made educational building for a medium-sized school. Six assembly rooms, eleven classrooms and many screens, curtains, blackboards, tables, cupboards, and so forth were provided at a cost of only about $2,000.

A beginning can be made with a single home-made screen. It will be tastefully decorated. It may even provide blackboard space on one side. Curtains and screens are rarely the ideal thing, but if nothing better can be secured they may be made to serve an excellent purpose. As compared with conditions often found in churches where possibilities of adaptation have not been closely studied, they are not to be despised. What a teacher needs is a reasonably good chance to teach. Toward that end small things have often been found to make great differences.

But who will see to it that these important small things are provided? Usually no one, unless the pastor is on the alert, or the general superintendent is especially keen and aggressive. Such details are not thought of by most people. It is only human to accept conditions as one finds them. Hence it will not normally enter the teacher's mind that adjustment of conditions is a part of the teaching function. He may be vaguely conscious that something is wrong; but inexperienced as he is in such matters, he does not know just where to look for the remedy. The pastor is not free from guilt if a prospectively good teacher is suffering on, week after week, under such a handicap. He should talk about it, telling what he has thought, and asking for opinions as to the value of a proposed adjustment; or, still better, he should talk with the superintendent and bring about a conference between the superintendent, the teacher and himself. If the approach has been directly to the teacher the pastor will of course have suggested that the teacher take the matter up with the superintendent; then the pastor and he can find a way to bring things to pass.

One very good reason why the pastor is needed in the task of improving equipment is that there often is difficulty about getting materials and getting work done, even after full agreement as to what is needed. He knows the constituency. He also, presumably, has a special influence with everyone, simply because of his place as pastor. If he takes with him a neat, even though amateurish sketch of the sort of thing he has in mind, he is sure to find the person who will give the small amount of necessary money for it; and to find the mechanic who will be glad to do the work as a service to his church. The project may not be taken so seriously, if it is not helped along by the backing of the pastor. Even though the general superintendent is on the aggressive, it will give strength to his mission if he can say: "The pastor has studied this problem with us and feels that this bit of equipment would substantially help along our work."

The number of things needing attention may be large. Perhaps a start will have been made with a few scattered items, nothing having been said about a general need. The slight improvements will have been shown to be of value, though of little cost. Other teachers will have noticed the improvement, or will have had their attention drawn to it by the enthusiasm of the one whose work has been made easier. The pastor may have suggested to those concerned that if they find the change has helped them, they tell the other teachers about the benefit they have experienced, inasmuch as people do not usually improve the conditions for their work unless they are *concerned* to have them improved, and can see just how this can be accomplished. Sometimes improvements can be handled as an enterprise of a class, or department, the pupils and teachers doing all or part of the work themselves. This may be a most excellent center of interest, and can be capitalized as a unit of work leading to scores of valuable " learnings " or " lessons " for the pupil. Especially if the group concerned is a young people's group, a wonderful opportunity is presented for the immediate development of a unit in leadership training, covering the problems: (1) What are we trying to teach? (2) Why do surroundings make a difference? (3) What are the conditions, or laws, of learning? (4) How should a good teacher teach?

The danger of such individual projects is, they may become selfish and all effort will be spent in improving one group. For example, Mrs. So-and-so's class of women decides to fix up their room, and they move heaven and earth—or even worse—throughout the entire church, to get this one room fixed up in an attractive manner; but in so doing they make it increasingly difficult to get anything done for the beginners, primary, or junior boys and girls. The same may happen with a young people's class, though the example is not likely to be so pronounced. The better plan, when there is a possibility of getting Mrs. So-and-so's class of women hard at work " fixing-up," would be to enlist them in an unselfish movement to meet the most urgent educational needs of the school in general. When that class of women, with their almost limitless possibilities, are in a mood to " fix something up," a pastor who does not know what are the needs of the school has not only let slip a great opportunity to improve his whole school, but has allowed full rein to the pagan principles " Do for yourself, and don't pay any attention to anyone else." Selfishness is innocently fostered all too generally in churches.

There are a hundred ways of improving the conditions of any school. Rarely does a month pass when a discerning eye does not see some point, however minor, at which something could be done both to give better chance to the teachers, present and future, and to teach something in the school and church while the improvement is being made. The very making of improvement is always to be understood as a teaching means.

But the pastor often becomes discouraged in his effort to lead in this sort of thing. He feels that people think of him as "always asking for something." That is not so bad as it would be for them to be able to say, "He never gets anything he asks for." He is there with the avowed purpose of leading these people to higher ground. Were he not to ask them for improvements, he would be more blameworthy than if he asked them for too many. His chief problem is to know when to ask, so as to ask wisely and successfully; and how to carry in his mind a list of needs-to-be-met. Under no circumstance must he forget what "grandmother said in her quaint old way," that "the world wasn't made in a day, a day!" Wisdom, clarity, tactful aggressiveness, patience—these finally win.

VIII

THE PASTOR FUNCTIONING IN THE ORGANIZATION

"Our church is not properly organized for Christian educational work," said a splendid business man to the writer. "I have just been chosen general superintendent of the Bible school and my pastor has suggested that I have a talk with you. There seems to be a readiness to study our whole organization and to try to put it in thoroughly good order. *What type is best?*"

1. The Best Organization

There is of course no out-and-out answer to this question. The best will always be the simplest, to meet the particular needs of each church; but the needs of each church are usually somewhat different from those of every other; and so it follows that the type of organization will be somewhat different in each case.

In this church there was not a readiness to study the whole situation. It was only the structure of the church school that was ready for a complete overhauling; the new general superintendent had not thought of the clubs, the missionary societies, the brotherhoods, the Scout troops, the young people's societies, and all the rest, as educational factors. He had thought of them as "auxiliary organizations"—which of course is less definitive than their original names. They really are all educational. They all teach something—often more than is realized. Had there been a thoroughly open mind on the part of all the leaders in the constituency of this church the answer would have been this:

Since it is obvious that all these organizations have an educational effect; since some are likely to duplicate the work with the same people in other organizations, while they have no contact at all with numerous others who are untouched, or nearly so, by any educational work of the church; and since our aim is helpfully to reach all, it is only good sense to make these facts increasingly clear to the whole church, and to authorize the simplest sort of central organization, to have supervision over the whole.

The pastor is logically the responsible head of the Christian educational work of the entire church constituency. But since his total ministry has so many ramifications, and since the Christian educational phase is in itself so vast, he needs two immediate agents to be associated with him: (1) A Christian education committee or board, to which is entrusted the responsibility of guiding the whole Christian educational program—study, recreation, worship, social program, service participation, etc.—of the church. This committee would be answerable to the entire educational fellowship of the church, meeting perhaps once a quarter. The educational fellowship would include the officers and teachers of the school, together with the ranking officer of each adult and young people's class, and the ranking officer of each auxiliary organization in the church. (2) A general superintendent of Christian education who will be not only the superintendent of the church school but also the delegated executive head of the entire Christian educational work. His specialized lieutenancy under the pastor is that of the educational program of the people. This being the case, the only educationally sound practice is for him to supervise the greatest possible number of educational influences that are about the lives of the persons being taught. He will in no sense displace or be in competition with the pastor. He will not make it any less necessary for the pastor to be expertly educationally minded. He will simply become a great brotherly partner of the pastor in the task of multiplying and extending the church's ministry. The pastor will be back of him, constantly advising, counseling, guiding, helping—delegating to him as much of the educational administration as conditions permit. The superintendent will not await orders. There will be an understanding between the pastor and him that the educational program is a more or less specialized phase of the work with which he is entrusted as delegated head, in much the same way as the music, finances or care of the building require each a delegated head.

Under the general superintendent there will be from four to a dozen departmental superintendents. If the church is small there might be good sense in extending the age-limit of a department superintendent's responsibility, putting under him, for example, the junior and intermediate groups; or the beginners' and primary group; or all of one department and part of another. But the normally best plan will be found to follow the established age-groupings, even though numbers may not be great. Each department superintendent will serve as under-superintendent, having jurisdiction over all the functions and activities of all in his department. This seems to the writer the most logical means of unification.

It does not imply that the church school will swallow up all the other organizations. It might be that all existing groups with their leaders would be continued exactly as they are. Indeed, more might be added. What is finally to be done about all such questions should be made a leisurely, practical, sympathetic and open-minded study on the part of the leadership and teaching staff of the particular age-group in question; counseling with parents, children, and anyone else with whom it may seem wise to counsel, the department superintendent being the responsible leader, and his staff being the authorized executive group for their department. They will make their decisions only after deliberate and prayerful search for divine guidance as to what is best for the spiritual well-being of the persons under their supervision. They will be slow to start new organizations, and still slower to kill present ones that have shown a continuing value. They will study the principle of adaptation, and use it as far as possible, not forcing issues where they do not need to be forced, but not neglecting actual needs. They will know and follow through every Christian relationship of each child, youth, or adult for whom they are accountable; seeing to it that the total experience of each is that of spiritual growth—constant and wholesome—in the directions indicated by the Seven Objectives quoted in Chapter I of this book. The only reason why the Sunday church school staff is suggested as the basis of unification is that it seems to be the most readily available. Here we actually find the people with whom it is our aim to deal.

We have come now to a very important point in our study, namely, the consideration of the instrument or instruments of unifying the Christian educational work of the church. Since it is so important let us try to summarize by means of these three propositions: *First, it is of great importance to coordinate, or, better still, to unify, the educational program of each age-group*. Overlapping and duplication at certain points in our educational effort, so that we come to have an actual competition at many points while at other points there is utter neglect, is henceforth to be regarded as sinful in the Christian church. There is no possible justification for it except on a basis such as *the Master would not approve*. It is of little concern to us just now whether we use the term "coordination" or the term "unification." The point is that the entire Christian educational program of each age-group should be studied from the angle of the total Christian experience of the persons in that group. If there are duplications that do not serve a really helpful purpose they should be overcome. If there are slighted areas, a plan should be devised for extending the good work to these areas, even though it may mean a rethinking of present accepted plans of work.

Secondly, since in the average church, the school is an organization independent of the church organization, and more or less parallel with other auxiliary organizations, it seems that the most effective immediate instrument of unification is a board of Christian education, created by the church, with the express function of guiding all Christian educational work in the direction of an intelligently unified program. This board, mark you, is the creature of the church, charged with special functions, namely: that of studying, planning, suggesting, carrying into effect a well-developed program of Christian education in the whole church constituency. The main reason why this special board is needed is that the school staff is at present charged only with the Sunday program and such activities as will gather around and supplement that program. All these activities tend at present to grow independently of what boys and girls, youths and adults, are doing through other organizations. There are tasks of studying personnel in the church school and other organizations; tasks of evaluating what is now being done and suggesting what ought to be done in the future. If this board can be made an intelligent, earnest, farseeing group, answerable to the church for their stewardship, they can be of great help. It will be necessary for them to be brave. Their task will be in many churches one of the most courageous imposed upon any board.

Thirdly, it is the writer's feeling that as adaptations are made in the total organization of the church looking in the direction of unification of program, there will come also a unification of staff, and that this unified staff will simply be an expansion of the school staff; in which case departmental staff meetings will come to be unified departmental staff meetings, and general staff meetings to be general unified staff meetings. We shall be happy to see that time; and if it comes we shall not be surprised to see the unified general staff take the place of a board of Christian education in the local church. In such a case it will be important to remember that the general staff and all under it will very likely take their authority from, and render their accounts to, and be absolutely adequately supported by, the church. They will enlist the entire church in a Christian educational program that will find its center in the entire church at worship, and they will not be satisfied with any plan that does not give a balanced program of work and service, graded to meet the interests of every age and temperament, and including adequate opportunities for study and for participation in Christian work of every description.

A full study of constitutions and church organizations is not here in place. Even the functions of a board of Christian education require a separate manual for their proper setting forth. Mutual understanding and simple effectiveness can be maintained by many methods. It is the results that count.

Before leaving the subject, it would seem to be in place to call attention to the fact that the organization of many of the churches with which one becomes acquainted is not such as to permit anything like the proper departmentalization of work and the proper distribution of responsibility in a thoroughly cooperative system. There are boards of deacons, deaconesses, trustees, music, missionary education—less frequently Christian education—but rarely a definition of the manner in which these boards cooperate, and no instrument by which these boards can plan their work together, thus coordinating or unifying the entire program of the church. In the larger churches something is needed in the way of a pastor's cabinet, composed of the heads of a few main departments under which the work of the church can be projected. It would seem that three main departments are enough: Finance (Trustees); Fellowship (Deacons and Deaconesses); and Education.

A cabinet—in fact any board—should not be too large. It is essential that such a cabinet should think and plan thoroughly and wisely. In recognizing the educational fellowship one should remember that there really are three natural *divisional* interests to be kept in mind: Children's Division, Young People's Division, and Adult Division.

2. Modifications of the Best Plan

Most churches would not be ready to centralize all their educational forces. What, then, is the next best type of organization? There is really nothing simpler than the various modifications of that which has here been described. The task is surveyed and divided along the lines that are discovered to be most natural, and then a person and the necessary assistants are commissioned to lead in getting that work done.

If the church is small the groups will all be proportionately smaller, but there is no reason why there need be any other modification. If it is large, they will be larger. The real question is not the size of the church or the groups, but the extent of educational supervision. In the case of the new superintendent with which this chapter opened it was needful finally to accept the fact that the church was not ready to unify its educational work under the church school departmental staffs. That really seemed like the sensible thing; but for local reasons it did not seem wise to have its jurisdiction extend further than the church school limits. The thing to do was to build a good church school, making an immediate mental note of the fact that the ultimate objective in any church is *an eduational church* —not merely a church with a good Sunday school and other auxiliary organizations functioning independently of each other. The mental note having been made, therefore, the thing to do was to develop the best possible work under existing circumstances; and every time a step could be taken looking toward a fuller realization of the ultimate objective, to take that step with as little ado as possible.

Toward the final attainment of that end a separate board of Christian education might have immediate value. It could be a small committee—three members, say, or it could be larger, including a group more representative of the varied educational factors in the constituency—the school among others. The function of this board would be that which has already been indicated.

3. The Pastor Fits In

In the majority of churches there will not be a paid staff. That is, there will not be a full-time office secretary, a full-time director of Christian education, a church visitor or professionally trained deaconess, and other assistants. More likely there will be none of these—or at most a versatile office secretary who may become sufficiently well-trained to adapt herself to some pastoral-assistant work. But whether the staff be paid, or volunteer, or both, there are two contentions modestly but persistently held to in all these studies: (1) The pastor must know the field of Christian education. There is no lively hope that the church can succeed in its educational work unless he does. (2) He must be the real head of the organization, his various lieutenants working unitedly under his leadership. Much of the work will be done through the lieutenants under the pastor's guidance.

A reason for many failures on the part of churches is that pastors have regarded the educational point of view as one in which they could specialize if they wanted to, or if they chose, could neglect; a purely optional matter. Such a view can no longer be held. It is of tragic importance that it be immediately corrected. There is no option about it. The pastor must be imbued with the point of view of Christian education, and deeply in sympathy with it, or his work is doomed to impermanence. Let it not be thought that by this statement there is intended any depreciation of a sane and wholesome evangelism. Evangelism, in the truer and wider sense, is the focal point toward which everything in the entire church program is directed. Lives are to be won to Christ, and are to be taught to observe all things whatsoever he hath commanded. The whole of this constitutes true evangelism.

Furthermore, the pastor should know his work in more than a superficial sense. He ought to be a philosopher of Christian education, so that he can look upon a new situation and accurately evaluate it on the basis of solid principles that can take the gaff of criticism from accepted public educational leaders. He may be the only person in his church who can meet on their own ground secular educators, interpreting to them the work in which the church is engaged. It is of great value to the work for him to be able to do this. If they dive down so deeply into the waters of educational philosophy that no one else can follow them, it is well to have at least one person around who can swim under water with them—and keep his eyes open while doing it—and know when to come up for air! Christian education must not be awed out of intelligent society by people who use big words, when those words often do not stand for true and valuable experiences. The pastor will help his community, his church and his fellow workers to understand these things as occasion arises.

He will always be earnestly trying to find a way properly to care for such seasonal work as the vacation school, the school of missions, or any new need that arises out of changing conditions. For the vacation school, at least, a permanent organization will be developed, functioning under the general sponsorship of the church school; but he will find the vacation opportunity so rich in possibilities that he himself will wish to keep close to it. Perhaps at times he will even personally direct it; or teach special groups.

Through the meetings of the education committee, or general staff, of the school, and through the various departmental staff meetings, he will make himself of value by means of definite suggestions looking ahead to the coming weeks and months. His knowledge of materials and speakers, of program themes and plans, will always be helpful. Knowing from experience how groups of people are most successfully led into a clarifying of their purposes and into the adoption as their own of the better thinking of others, he will make skilful suggestions as to how the technique of leadership can be improved. He will encourage the right sort of group-discussion and group-thinking; but will be very careful to point out the vast difference between real group-thinking and what one might better call "grope-thinking." While he will use the ideas of others, and encourage his leaders to do this, he will spread the idea among them that it is always wise for a leader to have something definite to suggest, if it develops that no one else has anything better. Everywhere and always he will avoid much speaking (for which in itself even the heavenly Father does not the more readily hear one); he will be a well-pleasing, friendly helper; not looking over anyone's shoulder in a spying manner, but standing by within easy reach when a real need arises. Thus they will turn to him again and again, and his satisfaction in being of help to so many will know no bounds.

IX

A BALANCED YEARLY PROGRAM

Twenty-five years ago the clergy of the liturgical churches were the chief, if not the exclusive, users of anything which approached a yearly schedule of church work. To them an annual program came as a natural accompaniment of the prescribed orders of worship, special feast days, seasons of catechizing and consecration, which made up the accepted "church year." Evangelical pastors felt it was important to guard against the perennial tendency in religion, first to become ritualistic, and then spiritually impoverished. The liturgical churches, they reasoned, constantly exposed themselves to this enervating virus.

The evangelicals were standing upon solid ground. There were these dangers. History had proven it. The Protestant reformation had been conducted on the basis of a proposition that was merely its restatement, namely, "justification by faith." But in their attempt to avoid the dangers of a stereotyped program by trusting always to the guidance of the Holy Spirit, the evangelicals found they were often falling into *the danger of stereotyping the Holy Spirit;* that is, they sought guidance from him; but month after month, judging from their monotonous work, he did not tell them to do anything other than that which they were already doing. So to devitalize the Holy Spirit amounted to the same thing as having a stereotyped program—if it was not even worse. The point at which their reasoning had gone astray was this: While they were right in holding that the Holy Spirit can, will and must direct one in the arrangement of each day's program and each week's program, they were wrong in acting upon the assumption that he cannot and will not and must not equally well direct one in the arrangement of an entire year's program—or for the matter of that, a program of two, or five, or fifteen years.

Certain evangelical pastors, as the years of their experience lengthened, came to this larger faith in the guidance of the Holy Spirit, and instituted in their work the practice of prayerfully planning for each year a balanced program looking throughout the entire twelve months. They did not use any the less the principle of seeking for each week and each day the will of the Spirit for that week and day. Often they found predetermined plans radically revised as there came some new leading touching the work of a given period; but even so, they found the yearly program putting into their work a greater vigor and definiteness of purpose, a more wholesome fruitage, than they had ever before known. They found their pastorates becoming stronger and more enduring than some others where a yearly program was frowned upon as unnecessary—if not an affront to the Holy Spirit.

As these evangelicals, who now believed the Spirit can see months as well as moments ahead, continued planning their programs, in the atmosphere of prayer, they finally noticed that year after year it was more easy and natural to do certain things when like things were being done by other churches in their community, or throughout all Christendom. Before they knew it they were timing and apportioning certain aspects of their work largely in accord with the timing and apportioning by the liturgical churches. Thus an increasing number of the more thorough evangelicals found themselves coordinating their work with that of the liturgists in spite of the fact that the basic reasoning of the former was quite different from that of the latter. The former built a program that would do as much as possible to induce a personal experience—salvation—the new birth and growth in grace; the latter trusted more largely the ability of the church to confer divine grace through approved instrumentalities sincerely devised for the purpose.

There is no point in here arguing the merits of the liturgists. These chapters are written especially for the evangelicals. All that we are trying to point out is that a sensible and adaptable church year is as needful and logical for the evangelicals as for the liturgists; that there really are seasons of the soul—times when all the conditions of the spiritual soil seem to be conducive to the sowing of the seed; others when germination and early growth seem most natural; others when the only thing to do is to continue stirring the soil and eliminating the weeds; others when blossoming and fruitage may be expected; and still others when the Lord of the harvest gathers the wheat, separating from it the tares, but preserving the good grain.

Taking into account all these factors and many others, though the evangelical is likely to think of his church year, from a practical angle, as beginning in the fall, one is inclined to be strongly impressed with the thought that there are three periods in the church year, and that the first of these periods should be thought of as beginning at Eastertime rather than in the autumn. The reason for such an interpretation is that it emphasizes more strongly the necessity of *planning work before it should begin.* Volume III, Number 2, of *The Evangel,* entitled "Year-Round Evangelism," is worthy of examination in this connection. The following is quoted from pages 12 to 14, inclusive:

The Church Year is Divided naturally into three parts: Easter to Autumn, Autumn to New Year's, New Year's to Easter. This division also coincides practically with our denominational year. And these are the three periods of the Year-Round Program. Mr. Strickland suggests that we emphasize during the first period the revival or revitalizing of the present church-membership; during the second period the rallying of the forces of the church for service, and during the third period making new disciples and preparing them for real fellowship in the church. We shall summarize the appropriate activities for each of these periods:

First Period (Easter to Autumn)—*Revitalizing the Church.* This will begin with an examination of the church's organizations and activities with a view to such changes as shall make them more useful toward the church's great evangelistic objective. A study of the church's problems will be made, such as the matter (1) of attendance; (2) of the quality of the worship service; (3) of standards for admission to church-membership and for continued fellowship in the church. During the First Period we shall give careful attention also to the follow-up of inactive members, who in most of the churches amount to almost half of the total membership. The Lord's Supper service, the most sacred and solemn experience in the church fellowship, may serve to stimulate attendance and reconsecration of those who have been careless of their Christian privilges. This is the time to set goals for attainment by Pentecost, and goals for the summer activities. Rev. H. D. Germer, of the Wilson Avenue Church of Youngstown, has the following objectives for post-Easter ministries outside of the regular activities of his parish: (1) To prepare and occupy a neglected farm, ten miles out of the city, for use by successive groups for camping and training during the summer. (2) To continue to develop his " Pleasant Friday Evenings " for boys and girls of a neglected neighborhood. (3) To open an out-station in such a neighborhood.

Second Period (Autumn to New Year's)—*Rallying the Forces of the Church.* After careful preparation (1) let the whole church assemble to hear the plans for advance presented by the representatives of each organization (whose program presumably was studied during the First Period). This assembly in the early autumn is a great occasion in some churches. (2) Make contacts with families that were discovered during the First Period and bring them into the congregation, then to Christ as Saviour, then into the membership of the church. (3) Discover other families through a religious census of some district near to the church—a district not so large but that the prospects may be followed up promptly and persistently. Evanston Church (Cincinnati) makes a census at regular intervals of only so much territory as they can cultivate promptly after the first call at the homes. (4) Hold one or more conferences of church workers that will consider such problems as Bridging the Gulf Between the Church and the Sunday School; How May the Sunday School Strengthen the Worship Service of the Church?

Third Period (New Year's to Easter)—*Winning the World to Christ and the Church.* Here the emphasis is upon ingathering. (1) Have ready lists of families secured during the Second Period, especially through the census and its follow-up. (2) Observe the week of prayer. (3) Select and instruct visitors and assign to them names for judicious use in visitation evangelism. (4) Intensify the evangelistic emphasis in all church activities as you come nearer to Easter. Include in your plans a Declaration Day in the Sunday school. Hold some special evangelistic services.

While the all but universal need of a yearly program has given birth to a number of excellent printed calendars with suggestions by dates, and while a number of these, if properly used, are possessed of real value, a vigorous and prayerful pastor will rarely receive more than suggestive help from them. He will prefer to make up his own program, after culling the best points from the printed ones and giving thorough study to the needs of his own field. If he does choose one of the printed programs and moderately adapts it, it will be one of the briefer type. To attempt to find an entire book that will serve as a week-by-week manual, a sort of inter-linear translation of his work, is for the pastor to beguile himself into lazy mental habits; and the price he will finally pay for that will be dullness. Most available manuals of the profuse type devote proportionately too much attention to the preaching and speaking work of the minister. They do not meet the need that is here being indicated. They might be used and yet in no way serve the purpose we are suggesting. *It is a Christian educational plan, that is needed,* with tentative objectives for each month; a plan which, at the end of a pastor's vacation, as he comes back to lead in another year's work, would be written on perhaps twelve pages in the back of his loose-leaf note-book.

He may, instead of using a page for a month's program (a line for each day), use a page for each week; though the former plan seems preferable, as it is less cumbersome and can more readily be seen in perspective. One of the nearest familiar approximations to such a thing is to be found in "A Calendar of Coordinated Denominational Activities," suggested for the use of churches of the Northern Baptist Convention. It is issued at 152 Madison Avenue, New York City, and is arranged for the year beginning September 1 and ending the following August 31. Even here there is much that would be disregarded, or rearranged, or adapted to local church needs, if particular attention is being given to Christian education. If the reader does not already have one of these in hand he would do well to secure and examine the last issue. He will notice that a large place is given to denominational interests; and advisedly so. Most pastors who are thorough in their work have long since discovered how valuable it is to cooperate closely in denominational aims and programs if a great impact is to be made upon a world of sin. They have also learned that much of the help offered by denominational leaders is of great assistance to the local pastor in doing more effectively the work of his own parish.

One of the commendable points of the particular Calendar above mentioned is that only the left half of each page is devoted to the printed suggestions, under the headings: Special Days; Activities; Meetings; and Founders' Days of Baptist Organizations. The entire right half of each page remains blank for the filling in of "Pastor's Notes." If more space is needed for this purpose—as is usually the case—it is a simple matter to cut the Calendar into loose leaves, punching holes for their insertion in the loose-leaf note-book, and placing between each two leaves an additional blank one.

In the average church an annual "retreat," or get-together

of some kind, is valuable for the purpose of considering the main objectives in the year ahead, and the final adoption of some major emphases and dates around which the work is to take shape. The adoption of objectives in advance serves to give the pastor greater confidence and power in leading. There is, however, this danger against which one must guard; there are some official groups that do not feel a thrill at "paper plans," worked out with nicety. Big propositions must be real; or it is probably just as well to let them grow step by step; the "paper plans" being kept in the pastor's own knowledge. As in every other case, what the minister does, and how much public attention is invited to what is going to be done, depend on the temperament of his official boards and the general constituency of his church.

Space limitations make it impractical to print here in full a sample program. It is assumed and urged that the reader will secure—if he does not already have—the one recommended, or another equally suited to his needs. Numerous suggestions will at once be crossed out. Preaching plans and subjects, prayer-meeting plans and subjects, special projects of many sorts, will be added; various board, cabinet and committee meetings will be scheduled; but the framework will have proven helpful.

A technique for program building may here be in place. The pastor who never before has laid out in advance the calendar of a year's work is apt to be bewildered as he sets himself to the task. The effort may be abandoned at the very start simply because one does not know just how to go about it. The following simple method has worked:

Since the plans for the coming year should use the discoveries of the past, and meet the felt needs of the present and future, it is well to first record on the left page of one's program-book three parallel calendars, devoting a column to each and having the dates of the month of the past year at the extreme left margin.

(1) Column one will be a simple listing, week by week, of the events that actually did take place during the last year. The pastor's date-book will show many of these. If a weekly *Bulletin* is used, the file, or the file and date-book together, will tell the story. These items need only to be copied, a word or two suggesting each activity.

(2) Column two will list opposite the proper dates the events and projects in the denominational and general church year. Information will come from such a denominational Calendar as is mentioned above. If one wishes to refer to the date of Easter or other "movable feasts" he will have in his library at least one volume clearly explaining *The Christian Year* and containing a table of such dates for the next twenty-five or fifty years.

(3) Column three will list in their proper allocation, according to date, the major items in the local church year, such as: the fall rally of forces; seasons for special emphasis upon leadership training; seasons for special emphasis upon decisionistic evangelism; the period for the stewardship or financial visitation; the time for the school of missions; the dates for the vacation church school; and the like.

With these three types of calendars in parallel columns it is a fairly simple task to prepare on the opposite page a synopsis for the projecting of each enterprise, giving plans, leaders and dates for *the coming year*. Such a synopsis will also reveal the fact that some items and projects need to be unified. If one does not wish to go to the extent of rewriting the entire program in one synopsis he can use the materials just as they are developed to this point. A better plan, however, is to rewrite, having the new program on one page and the story of last year's program on the opposite page for reference.

After the first year the program-building process will be much easier, and from year to year it will become increasingly so.

Whether the pastor thinks of his church year as starting immediately after Easter or with the coming of autumn he will be conscious of the fact that September first must see a well-prepared program of work "ready to go." Modern conditions make it essential that the world's aggressiveness shall be matched and surpassed by a Christian aggressiveness that is carefully thought out and in a definite form. This program of work will apply to every aspect of church and school: educational, financial and organic (that is, having to do with membership and organization), and it will reach to all phases of the church's life. In all but the most unusual situations the summer period is rather hard on churches. With the coming of early fall, new members of the previous year or two need all to be carefully "checked" to see whether their Christian lives are growing as they should. A great danger to which evangelicals are subject is that they will neglect the encouragement of growth in grace. We mean well, but are somewhat careless of details which may prove of eternal importance. The rally of the educational fellowship is vital. The customary and obvious means will be used, but in each case there will be a searching and determined purpose to give character to it—to quicken its spirit. In the twentieth century results do not just happen. There are causes back of them, divine and human. Especially Rally and Promotion Days can be made to serve an educational purpose; but not unless planned and magnified toward that end. Prospects and enrolments will of course be pushed.

October and November have special building-up possibilities. Seasonal themes will be appropriately used. Pastors often fail to see the necessity of beginning in this period the activities looking toward a wise guidance of the decisionistic aspects of evangelism. A sane evangelism cannot be conducted in only two or five weeks of the year. It must be educational as well as decisionistic, and must reach through the year. October is the time to begin putting plans into effect if mistakes are to be avoided six months later. It is also the golden month in which to see that plans are on foot for the year's leadership training program. These will have been projected earlier in the fall, but by now must be actually moving.

A valuable children's program, or better, family program, needs to be set in motion at this time. Many of us have the feeling that something like the unified service, as described by Beaven in *Putting the Church on a Full-Time Basis* is destined to come into far more common usage. Such a thing cannot be immediately set up, however, and as its description is readily available extended space need not here be given to it. If a church does not feel ready to make the special study and adjustment necessary for the inauguration of so radical an innovation as this, a compromise program of simple character can be set up in October, looking through five or more months:

The idea is to encourage the habit of family attendance upon public worship by planning a wholesome children's program in connection with the morning worship. During the first seven weeks all junior and primary boys and girls are especially urged to come and sit with their parents or teacher (far preferably the parents) for the first twenty minutes of the public worship. Attempt is made to present an educationally sound children's story with but little, if any, comment; and have the remainder of the opening service of a definite public worship character, in view of the presence of families *as families.* The second hymn is a recessional for the boys and girls to go to departmental work, using the standard missionary educational material for Heralds and Crusaders, or using extra session material which is now available in connection with the Keystone Graded Series. If the former material is used it will be the Foreign book during the first seven weeks. The second seven weeks (or perhaps even *ten* weeks) family attendance is again stressed, but by prearrangement small blank-page booklets with attractively colored covers have been prepared, and a series of pictures from the Perry or Hammond houses, selected on the basis of their teaching value. Having secured enough of each of these to give each child who is willing to follow through the work, attending services with parents and seeking their help in the work, the pastor selects for each picture two children and has them come to the parsonage in groups of from six to ten. As they sit together in the study he gives them each an idea of the work they are to do. Wilma is to prepare a little story about the picture "The Last Supper." She will tell who painted it and about its "message." What does it mean? The pastor will help and her parents will help find materials. They will talk about it at table—perhaps even purchase a large print of it for their home. The "essay," when written will be printed or mimeographed in the bulletin for the Sunday when that picture is scheduled, but printed in such shape as to allow clipping it out and pasting it on a page of the booklet. Robert will take the same picture, but have his parents help him select from five to eight appropriate verses of Scripture to further explain or interpret the picture. Thus two will be put at work on each picture. Parents will begin to ask more details. These questions will be the occasion of valuable pastoral contacts. Jean, Catherine, William, Franklin and all the others—two for each Sunday—are deeply interested. Their parents, relatives and close acquaintances are being enlisted. On the morning when "The Last Supper" is to be used—Communion Sunday—after the dignified opening worship, in an atmosphere of perfect quiet and without announcement (for names and explanations have previously been attended to in the printed or mimeographed bulletin), Wilma comes forward and stands beside a framed copy of the picture and reads or tells what she knows of the picture. Following this, but without any announcement, Robert comes forward (they have gone into the pulpit with the pastor, after prayer together in the study), and recites or reads the Scripture verses. After the last verse the organ starts a carefully selected hymn, posted but not announced, and the congregation join in one of the deepest worship experiences they are capable of having. There is no show-off about it. It is so conducted as to eliminate this. There is no laughter, but there *are* plenty of moist eyes. Relatives are in the church that morning who have not been present for some time; and the service has taken hold upon them. Splendid by-products from a plan of this kind are many and far-reaching. The next seven weeks will go back to the plan of the first seven, except that, if the missionary education material is used, it will be the Home instead of the Foreign text. It is the writer's opinion that if the child-loving and child-understanding Saviour were planning this work he would use during this extra session a large proportion of material enlisting the activities, the participation, the manual and even play expressions of the boys and girls. He would not be a bit hesitant about manual activities that are really educational simply because it is Sunday. His preeminent purpose would be to teach them the way of eternal life.

Unusual space has been given to the description of the foregoing unit of interest in order to suggest how a very simple thing can branch out in many useful directions and become a major item in the Christian education program of the year. As a matter of fact that is what happened in this case. For many months reverberations of gratitude and of stirrings of heart were coming from numerous homes. There is no possible reason for not doing such a simple thing unless there is a better and more serious plan on foot. The fact is, the entire family must be captured for Christ, or we are likely to lose even those members from the family who have shown interest. The more frequently one can make a really natural appeal to the family, the better. For example, in some churches whenever a person is baptized the family are asked to be present in the congregation and stand while one of their members is being baptized. Fine! One of the major items in each church year should be a constructive program directed toward the family and its religious function.

Concerning the Christmas season it need not even be suggested, one would suppose, that the Christmas pageant, if reverently conducted, is the logical high point around which the month's Christian educational work can well be arranged. In one church there are few Christmas pageants that do not witness some known spiritual experience of a rather deep character, and doubtless many which do not come directly to the pastor's personal knowledge. In this case the pastor himself gives direction to the pageant. Something more than a hundred people from all branches of the church take parts appropriate to their respective ages. The "White Gift" feature is the fitting accompaniment of the pageant.

The writer has found it of value to make the Sunday marking the anniversary of the beginning of his pastorate an occasion for summarizing and evaluating the past and for the indication of emphases that need next to be made. Such things aid in giving direction to a pastorate. If the use of so personal an anniversary does not appeal to one, there is the New Year Sunday, which naturally lends itself to "giving an account of one's stewardship." It is also a good thing to have annually some sort of Founders' Day, of the Sunday school or church, when the best traditions of the church are educationally interpreted. If this should fall not too long after the annual selection of the various educational leaders, it will be an appropriate time for a carefully planned installation service. The sermon, by the local pastor or by a special speaker, will be on some appropriate aspect of Christian education in the local church.

In the evangelistic program an increasing number of pastors are finding it of value from January to Easter to recognize and use the Lenten emphasis of the Christian world. "Christian life classes" are conducted for instruction in the meaning of the Christian life and church membership. Less than five sessions is not enough. The pastor will personally teach the third-year juniors, and arrange for other special meetings with selected groups of intermediate young people and adults. The classes should begin about seven weeks before Easter; and it seems especially well to encourage baptisms of those who are sincere week by week from January 1 to Easter—and then encourage a continuance *after* Easter!

It may be in place before going further to recognize a feeling on the part of some that the so-called Lenten period should not too habitually be used as a time for the encouragement of baptism and uniting with the church. The reasons given are: (1) That public profession of Christ by a few should be coming every month rather than by the overwhelming majority in a few weeks; and (2) Those who come *with* others and presumably in part *because* of the coming of others are likely not to have had a real personal Christian experience. There is little use in attempting the point-blank denial of the worth of either of these reasons. Each states a grave danger against which there must be the most eternal vigilance. Yet concerning the first it will have to be admitted that, human nature being what it is, it seems almost inevitable that there will be times when the Spirit works among greater numbers than at other times. Pentecost and all sincere revivals are examples of the same thing. The making of decisions should be a natural thing at any time and should be constantly encouraged; but it can hardly be right to discourage the coming of groups, if they have given reasonable evidence of reality of purpose. Concerning the second reason it should be noticed that it really is not, after all, a matter of the season of the year. It is a matter of the superficial testing of the new convert at any time. Anyone who is swept into the church without the most careful testing of the impelling motives is subject to this defect. The point to stress, then, is simply that we must be as careful as is humanly possible that the Christian experience is real. That is all we can do, be it summer or winter, Yuletide or Lent. It is not a question of seasons or numbers but of the individual's spirit. Whatever seasonal interests can be used should be used; and then special vigilance should be employed to safeguard sincerity.

If many persons have united with the church during the Lenten period, one of the most significant periods of the year, educationally, will be the months immediately following Easter. For each new member a "pal" will be assigned—an older member—who will closely follow this new member and see that he or she is properly injected into the life of the church. There must be no possibility of their thinking, as so many do, "You *join* the church, and that is all there is to it." It is only a step in an endless process that has many high experiences along the way.

The wise pastor will not forget graduations in June; nor will he overlook the importance of the vacation school, which must be ready to start in July. Perhaps he will personally direct it. The July schedule is not so heavy in some other respects and very likely has more educational possibilities by means of such a center as the vacation school. His active participation in the work is a means of keeping him informed and alive educationally. When he turns to his own vacation it will be in a frame of mind well-fitted for the completion of his program for the coming months. Vacations are for physical recuperation and the storing up of reserve strength; but they are also poorly planned if they are not used as a means of storing up a reserve of intellectual and spiritual strength as well. There is nothing better in this respect than well-planned reading and study, coupled with the building of the outlines of the year's education program. A prepared program is in itself a storehouse of strength. It will save scores of hours of floundering during the year and an unmeasurable amount of nervous energy that would otherwise be burned up in uncertainty and worry.

A pastor is very blind to the possibilities of his own growth if he does not carefully plan and use a vacation that will serve as a time of retirement for special study, calculated to enrich his ministry so that each year he will be a better preacher and an abler leader than he was the year before. Likewise, a church that does not insist on arranging for its pastor taking such a substantial period of retirement each year for this use is impoverishing its own life and limiting its own channels of blessing by cutting off the possibility of certain enrichments which can readily be had.

To be sure, there are a few pastors who do not know how to use a vacation. For such it might well be made a matter of yearly habit to talk over with some of their leaders the manner in which this enrichment can best come. If people knew in what field their pastor was seeking, in retirement, to enrich his own life, their interest in this field might be especially kindled and the coming year might find them watching and listening for the new elements of worth that have come from the hills, unto which in days of old the psalmist so frequently lifted up his eyes.

X

KEEPING THE THRILL

All over the land there are pastors who have somehow lost the zest of their work. Once the vision glorious was theirs. They achieved splendidly. But the day came when the battle grew too fierce, the mountain too steep; and something terribly important went out of their soul. They even wondered whether their high faith in the ministry might not have been misdirected. In school days, when they were studying the Christian educational materials available for use in the local church, it seemed so simple and thrilling to change human nature. The triumphant lives of the great preachers; the basic theology and philosophy back of the gospel; the well-known technique of sermon structure; the story of the glorious company of the apostles and of the ultimately victorious march of the church universal—it was all as though the whole creation was proclaiming the power of the ministry for the conquest of the human heart.

In those days, however, the roughness of the lonely road which the prophet must often travel apparently had been forgotten. When the experience came, month after month, it either brought a chronic lump to the throat, or it so convinced them of the unfairness of life that they reconciled themselves to the private acceptance of the maxim upon which the overwhelming majority of worldlings (and even churchlings) seem to act—"Do as well as you conveniently can, but in a pinch look out for yourself, first, and consider the principles of the situation afterward." When either of these things has happened in the heart of a pastor it is a dark and disastrous day for his church. No matter what may be the cause of the discouragement the leadership ability of that pastor now hangs more upon his power of spiritual recuperation—his power for recapturing the thrill—than upon anything else. The sources from which the enemies of ministerial faith burst forth are numerous and varied: Humanity's slowness to comprehend the gospel teaching; or, having comprehended it, to follow its mandates; the unwillingness of all but a few to share open-mindedly and open-heartedly the everlasting work and self-discipline essential in the function of Christian educational leadership; personal rebuffs from individuals or groups in the church, upon whom the pastor has counted implicitly, but who, under pressure, do not measure up; ill-health, and the inability to find the strength to lead on in the arduous program; that which Harold Bell Wright years ago designated as "The Ally"—the poisoned tongues of thoughtless people whose idle words hurt both him and the work; and a thousand other things which the originality of each field seems to develop according to its own temper. But whatever may be the sources of these enemies, or whatever their justification, if they succeed in battering down his faith—the devil has temporarily won in his life and pastorate.

The fact is, the ministry calls for a stout heart and a great deal of self-possession. How shall these be achieved and expanded?

The cultivation of the private devotional life may be an old prescription, but at least it is tried and it is true. No one person can tell another just how to build his altar; what to read and when; what posture to assume; what words to use; and what times—in prayer. But it may be asserted with practical dogmatism that the person who does not in his own way find the place and manner of erecting his altar is not likely to maintain for many years the enjoyable thrill that is necessary for a contagious and fruitful Christian work. It is not a question of one's theology; but of one's experience. When he has gone into his inner chamber and shut to the door, he must be able to commune with his Father who seeth in secret; and have the experience of being rewarded "openly." One's preaching and pastoral leadership often seem to pass through desert places chiefly because one is not himself "dwelling on the mountain, underneath a cloudless sky," or "drinking at the fountain that never shall run dry." Here and there throughout the country a community suddenly awakens to the fact that they have within their midst a minister who *deeply and profoundly believes what he is saying and working at.* None of them—or at most few of them—really disbelieve. But the belief of many seems to be rather "after the hearing of the ears." Suddenly there dawns upon folks a realization that here is one who has a *deep experiencing of the heart.* This thing he is teaching *is true!* It seems as though he must talk it and preach it and live it, *everywhere! It is actually true!*—And unless that thrill has come to him, he is poor indeed. If it *has* come, he is essentially irrepressible. He can lead in the conquest of the world for Christ; for the conquest has actually begun in his own heart.

But what then? Will it all come easily? Will the world rush to his doors, or to his church? By no means! He must cultivate a clear mind and a growing mind. His field of work is without limit. No ten men in an entire lifetime could master it all; how much less himself, alone, in so short a time as he has! As a sheer defense against spiritual weakness he will guard his reading schedule. His time is precious. He will learn how to read—studying certain chapters or books and only scanning others; allowing book reviews to suffice for many a volume, or racing in an hour madly through one, leaping from high spot to high spot; and then turning to the more solid type of material and studying laboriously every word and phrase. Fog is always bewildering, and none more devastatingly so than intellectual and spiritual fog. The minister must have an ever-increasing flood of the sunlight of knowledge and inspiration pouring into his life from the pens of the good and great. Prof. Walter Rauschenbusch wrote in 1918 a few suggestive sentences in this connection, interpretive of his own experience:

> Far away on a wind-swept height my soul has built her a castle, whither she retreats from the strife of men, and when the great gate swings to its lock, my soul is well-content with its company.
>
> For in the painted hall, under the groined arches, she has supped with great men. Isaiah has chanted to her in Hebrew, and Plato has discoursed in Attic, and many an historian has lifted the fringe of the Curtain of Seemly Lies that wraps the Book of Reality.
>
> Springing from the west wall, and overhanging the pleasant Valley of Dreams, is the Balcony of Laughter. Here Walther von der Vogelweide told of the song of a certain nightingale, and Horace strummed in Sapphic measure to the eyebrows of Lalage, looking thirstily for the cool joy of Falernian, and finding it not.
>
> High above the castle, stretching into the starry infinity, is the watch tower of my soul. Thence she looks down on the kingdoms of this world and wants not their glory; and forward to the Things That Shall Be; and up to the sickle of Venus, and the rings of Saturn, and the belt of Orion, and the glorious locks of Cassiopeia, and my soul leaps to the Milky Way, bounding from star to star, where God strode down through Eternity when the morning stars sang to Him in the Youth of the World.
>
> But beneath the castle is a dark corridor, which my soul would fain forget and cannot. However softly she steals past, ghosts creep forth, crying softly, and bidding her remember how she trampled on trust and love in blind ignorance or blinder anger. And she remembers. This is the castle of my soul, and when my soul has locked the gate, her nearest kin lives 10,000 leagues away.

But neither the knowledge which comes from books nor that which comes directly from the warm lives of people will automatically guide his work. He must use the appropriate instruments of systematization. The worth of many a Christian education program has been saved from ruination or moved from a position of mediocrity to one of power by the exceedingly simple discovery of how to "organize oneself in leatherette." A minister would have to have a secretary constantly at his call if he were to develop an extensive set of personal records and files. Loose-leaf note-books, however, do not need to be either expensive or voluminous, provided one has arrived at the beginning of a well-considered system, on the basis of which to organize and preserve in classified form the bulk of his work. Vertical file materials are now so well developed and so perfectly adaptable to every sort of work that there is no good excuse for not using them. They constitute a type of equipment upon which it almost seems the entire modern world is run. How can a pastor hope to avoid despondency if in his work he does not make use of the most effective instruments of warfare used by the enemy. A young man should not be permitted to graduate from a theological seminary or school of Christian education if he has not demonstrated his acquaintanceship with and his ability to adapt to his work the various types of filing cabinet in common and specialized use and the various types of folder and loose-leaf materials, with their differently colored tabs, and all the rest. If this aspect of one's training has been neglected, it can be superficially acquired by a single visit to a really good office where a specialization is made of files and loose-leaf systems. In a few hours of time a start on a system will have been made, and by the end of two years the pastor will be using it and developing it according to his needs, with splendid effect and increasing joy. His task will take on a new zest. He has been overwhelmed by work that was simply too complicated for him to systematize without mechanical aids used by others.

The problem of the pastor in maintaining his morale is partly that of keeping himself engaged not with trifles, but with important and creative things. Which things really are important no one else in the entire church is so fitted as himself to judge. Many important things do not come up in the ordinary routine, and are therefore on no docket if not on his. Some of his finest thrills come from the saving of opportunities that, but for his attentive eye and hand, would be completely lost. He " organizes himself " in order to know when he is following up " unfinished business " and when he is putting forward " new business."

Yet, with it all, he will often be tempted to become weary of the everlasting day-in-day-out work which is so rarely attended by any clear public demonstration of " results achieved." The sensationalist has the temporary satisfaction of seeing a crowd come to the church. The popular evangelist may be cheered on his way by the number of his converts. At the very least, he will have the satisfaction of seeing the soil of the human heart stirred to an unusual depth and the interest of the community awakened by newspaper and other discussion. The man who bends all his efforts toward " popular preaching services "—and attains them at the expense of everything else —will at least revel for a year or two in the appreciation of many in his church who " like to see results "—though they do not critically evaluate the sort of " results " they are commending. The work, however, of a pastor who does not dissipate his own and the energies of others in sensationalism or sentimentality, but rather tries to build his whole pulpit and pastoral ministry around the principles and spirit of Christian education, does not seem to have a great amount of showiness about his work. Showiness is what the general public likes. Showiness, to the non-discriminating mind, is " results." But even so, the educationally minded pastor can gradually teach his inner circle that the true measure is not at all in this realm, and under no circumstance will he allow himself to indulge in the use of superficial standards.

He will see the lives before him and judge what is really happening to them in an eternal sense. He will think of their worth—of their infinite possibilities—and will try to direct them *as they ought to be directed.* He will think frequently of the fact that, regardless of human judgments, the day comes for everyone when his life's work is ended, and having crossed the swelling tide, he alone stands before the judgment-seat of God. God is love, but even so God is also a judge—a great kindly Judge—knowing all the opportunities every one has had, whether he has sold out to selfishness, or vanity, or passion, or anger, or fretfulness, or any other of the transitory things. The great Judge will know whether he was able to stand truly, and lead wisely and gently. And so at each bedtime moment, as the pastor kneels as he has always knelt, since childhood, it will be with fatigue upon his body, the sense of willing sacrifice in his heart, the iron of heroism in his spirit, but also with the "lump" of thankfulness and satisfaction in his throat. "And the cares that infest the day shall fold their tents like the Arabs, and as silently steal away."

> "Toiling—rejoicing—sorrowing,
> Onward through life he goes;
> Each morning sees some task begun,
> Each evening sees it close.
> Something attempted, something done,
> Has earned a night's repose."

FURTHER READING

Long reading lists are purposely omitted from this brief study. Bibliographies in Christian education, like those in most other fields, in recent years have become very repetitious. It is recommended that the student secure either the study lists from his own denominational leadership training headquarters, or almost any one of the more recent text-books for use in community and local church training schools. A book on Supervision would perhaps be the best with which to begin. Frank M. McKibben's *Improving Religious Education Through Supervision* is to the point. It is full of help. After each chapter will be found a generous list of books covering various fields.